Hawaii No Ka Oi

THE KAMIYA FAMILY TRILOGY

Edward Sakamoto

FOREWORD BY FRANKLIN S. ODO

UNIVERSITY OF HAWAI'I PRESS, HONOLULU

Hawai'i No Ka Oi: The Kamiya Family Trilogy © 1995 by Edward Sakamoto. Foreword © 1995 by University of Hawai'i Press.

Hawaii No Ka Oi (short versions of *Manoa Valley* and *Aala Park*) © 1980 by Edward Sakamoto

Manoa Valley © 1981, *The Life of the Land* © 1981, *The Taste of Kona Coffee* © 1993 by Edward Sakamoto

All rights reserved   Printed in the United States of America

00 99 98 97 96 95   1 2 3 4 5

Library of Congress Cataloging-in-Publication Data

Sakamoto, Edward, 1940–
  Hawai'i no ka oi : the Kamiya family trilogy / Edward Sakamoto ;
foreword by Franklin S. Odo.
    p.   cm.
  Contents: The taste of Kona coffee — Manoa Valley — The life of the land.
  ISBN 0–8248–1726–5 (acid-free paper)
  1. Kamiya family (Fictitious characters)—Drama. 2. Japanese American families —Hawaii—Kona (Hawaii Island)—Drama. 3. Japanese Americans—Hawaii— Kona (Hawaii Island)—Drama. 4. Domestic drama, American—Hawaii— Kona (Hawaii Island) 5. Coffee trade—Hawaii—Kona (Hawaii Island)— Drama. 6. Family—Hawaii—Kona (Hawaii Island)—Drama. I. Title.
PS3569.A45459H39   1995
812'.54—dc20   95–21472
                                                                                                          CIP

Cover illustration: (Top) September 1993 world premiere of the Kumu Kahua production of *The Taste of Kona Coffee*, directed by James A. Nakamoto, at Tenney Theatre. *From left:* Karen Yamamoto Hackler as Mikame, Marcus Oshiro as Aki, Devon Nekoba as Tosh. (Photo by Joseph D. Dodd.) *(Bottom):* April 1982 world premiere production of *Mānoa Valley*, directed by Glenn Cannon, at Kennedy Theatre, University of Hawai'i at Mānoa. *From left:* Darryl Tsutsui as Nobu, Stan Egi as Tosh, Kati Kuroda as Tomi, Suzanne Park as Laura, Mitchell Young as Toku. (Photo by Malcolm S. Mekaru.)

University of Hawai'i Press books are printed on acid-free paper and meet the guidelines for permanence and durability of the Council on Library Resources

Designed by Kenneth Miyamoto

*This trilogy is dedicated to the memory of my
parents, Jitsuichi and Masako (Hatakeyama) Sakamoto,
who grew up on Kona coffee farms.*

Contents

Foreword
Can You Go Home Again?
by Franklin S. Odo
ix

Acknowledgments
xxvii

Production Credits
xxix

THE TASTE OF KONA COFFEE
1

MĀNOA VALLEY
49

THE LIFE OF THE LAND
91

Glossary
139

FOREWORD

Can You Go Home Again? Edward Sakamoto's Plays and Japanese Americans in Hawai'i

FRANKLIN S. ODO

PUBLICATION OF THIS COLLECTION of Edward Sakamoto's plays marks an important step in the development of American theater. It will be of particular interest to students of the modern history of Hawai'i and the Japanese American experience.[1] It will also attract the attention of people concerned with Asian American culture and arts as well as race relations in general. Most specifically, these plays will be of great interest to individuals following the resurgence of Asian American theater.[2]

All immigrants brought their own languages and theater forms to Hawai'i and the United States mainland. The Japanese in Hawai'i, for example, sponsored touring troupes from Japan and established theaters for traditional Kabuki as well as modern (*shinpa*) plays as early as 1900.[3] More recently, the staging of plays by Asian American playwrights dealing with Asian American experiences has been extremely important, especially in regional theaters ranging from Honolulu and Seattle to San Francisco and Los Angeles as well as in New York City. Ed Sakamoto has had numerous works performed in these venues, but publication will make his plays more widely accessible to the general public.

With the completion of *The Taste of Kona Coffee*, the earliest of the Kamiya family history, we now have a trilogy that provides a substantial body of theater on the experiences of Japanese Americans in Hawai'i. These are plays intended for the stage and are obviously best appreciated when produced. As scripts, they need to be read carefully, with the playwright's directions and a good measure of the readers' active imagination to suggest the drama and comedy implicit in the action and tableaux.

Reading these plays is well worth the effort because they are superb depictions of real and vital characters rooted in place and time. In this introductory essay, I hope to provide the social and political context of that place and time. I will also discuss the language used in the plays; we in Hawai'i call it "Pidgin," but it is a distinct language that linguists call Hawaiian Creole English (HCE). Because I find the plays so valuable as vehicles to critique stereotypes of Japanese Americans, I explore concrete examples of cultural values that are routinely and, in my view, mistakenly attributed to this group. I also include background information on Ed Sakamoto as a developing writer. Much of my interpretation is based on personal reflection as well as traditional scholarship.

Historical Background

As a result of Sakamoto's craft, we are afforded intimate insights into one family's confrontation with the changing world of Hawai'i in the half century between 1929 and 1980. Sakamoto allows us to watch the immigrant Japanese, the issei, in Kona on the Big Island of Hawai'i, as they struggle to survive in a difficult setting. The hard work involved in grappling with nature to make it yield rich coffee beans is relatively easy compared to an economic system clutching them in a semifeudal relationship to large landowners and coffee mills.

The Taste of Kona Coffee is set in 1929 and reveals the nisei Kamiya children grown into two young men as they attempt to break away, leaving for the tantalizing world of urban Honolulu. In the process, Aki and Tosh learn about their neighbors and even come to appreciate something of the world inhabited by their immigrant parents who barely manage a hardscrabble existence. The American-born sons must free themselves from the twin constraints of old-world traditions as well as neocolonial economic and sociopolitical bondage.

In *Mānoa Valley*, which takes place in 1959, the two sons have achieved a modest measure of individual success and can dream of passing on a life of relative ease to their own boys. Aki has become a successful landscape nursery owner, but his son has no intention of continuing the business. Instead, he dreams of becoming a politician. Tosh, the younger brother, is now a prosperous building contractor, happily preparing a party to celebrate the attainment of statehood for Hawai'i. He discovers, however, that his son, Spencer, is being drawn to the more exciting world of mainland America. Tosh must now face the confrontation between his cherished dream in which Spencer inherits the company and his son's own ambitions.

The Life of the Land brings us to 1980 and explores the dilemma of the "successful" third-generation sansei, who ponders the price of his sojourn on the mainland. Spencer wonders whether he can ever go home again. He has achieved his goals but regrets all he has left behind, especially the family ties. His cousin is still pursuing dreams of elected office, although by 1980 the original reform ideals of Japanese Americans and the Democratic Party are badly shaken by cronyism, self-satisfaction, and arrogance.[4]

Sakamoto's plays cover a critical period. *The Taste of Kona Coffee* is set in a Hawai'i ruled by a tightly knit, intermarried, interlocking, oligopoly of white families who control a handful of corporations called the Big Five. Their ownership of sugar and pineapple provide power over everything from banking, insurance, and other financial services to utilities, retailing, and the critical shipping industry. This control of Hawai'i's economic base extended to overwhelming influence over the political, communications, educational, and social spheres of life in the Islands.

> The entire system operated along the racist lines established by the plantation interests in the mid-nineteenth century, when a cultural division of labor had been imposed upon sugar production to facilitate exploitation of (and to divide) the proletariat. A somewhat different cultural division of labor was maintained throughout the pre-Pearl Harbor era: Chinese were found in small businesses, Japanese in small businesses, on small farms, and on plantations, Portuguese were plantation foremen and skilled crafts people, Filipinos were plantation laborers, and Hawaiians were low-level government workers, stevedores, and construction workers.[5]

Noel Kent has argued, persuasively, that this ruling elite was both supported by and dependent upon far more powerful capitalist entities in the metropolitan centers of the U.S. mainland.[6] This was a society, partly as a result of its historically fragile dependency relationship, on the verge of major shifts in political economy and social stratification. The seemingly unending stream of profit from sugar was, after all, the result not only of abundant lands stolen from Native Hawaiians and cheap imported labor from Asia but of a protected market in the United States. And, in the national context, the Territory of Hawai'i was far too small to play any major role except as a military and strategic bulwark against the threat of Japanese competition in the Pacific. When Japan attacked Pearl Harbor in December 1941, Hawai'i was thrust into a maelstrom of change.

World War II and the immediate postwar years transformed the demography forever and, ironically, empowered the Japanese American population beyond any dream they might have had in 1929.⁷ The emergence of a powerful International Longshoremen's and Warehousemen's Union (ILWU), along with the return of thousands of Japanese American veterans, changed the political landscape. Land development and tourism overtook sugar and pineapple as principal industries, although "the transformation of the old *kamaaina* [in this case, the traditional white elite] corporate complex in Hawai'i from local sugar agencies to medium-sized transnational corporations with far-reaching interests has *not*—contrary to prevailing wisdom—acted as a force for genuine economic development and political liberation in Hawaii."⁸

The end result was a society still fundamentally peripheral to and dependent upon larger capitalist forces in some distant metropolis. The Big Five corporations were forced to sell off landholdings in selected areas for resort and development purposes. Eventually, giant financial and construction institutions from Japan and the mainland United States absorbed the local Big Five. In this sense, as Kent has argued, the larger context of political power remained largely the same. But the precise mix of forces underwent considerable change, and the new configuration was of profound importance to the lives of families like the Kamiyas, who found far more opportunity for their entrepreneurial energy after the end of World War II.

The social and political contexts are critical to understanding Sakamoto's plays. The rise of a militant union movement, the transformation of the economy from industrial agriculture to tourism and federal dependency, and the ascendance of the Democratic Party in the mid-1950s are in the distant background. The power of the ILWU made it possible for large numbers of agricultural workers to secure decent wages and working conditions as well as entertain realistic hopes for better lives for their children. The economic and political gains made thereby are difficult to overstate; they made possible more educational and entrepreneurial opportunities for nearly an entire class of working people, including the Kamiya family. The increased wages of the plantation families permitted their children to pursue educational opportunities in ways and numbers not previously imagined. At the same time these families were able to buy and build houses or businesses that sustained the nurseries and construction companies developed by the dozens of real-life counterparts of Aki and Tosh.

The post–World War II economic boom, coupled with the advent of affordable jet travel, catapulted Hawai'i into the ranks of the most desirable vacation destinations. At the same time, Hawai'i's strategic position became even more valuable as the United States emerged from World War II as the world's most powerful nation and undisputed ruler of the vast Pacific region. Finally, all of these forces combined to help the Democratic Party forge a new set of alliances, which, in 1954, unseated the Big Five-dominated Republicans who had ruled uninterrupted for over half a century—since Hawai'i had become a territory.

This background is important for a full and rich understanding of Sakamoto's plays, although he is not primarily concerned with history lessons and remains firmly focused on the family. This history helps us understand, for example, the Kamiya family's upward mobility. Parts of Mānoa Valley were opened up for development as a new middle class of Asian Americans was provided with the means, for the first time in Hawai'i's history, of purchasing their own modest homes. It is entirely reasonable, therefore, for Sakamoto to situate his 1959 play in Mānoa and to appropriate the valley's name for the title of his play. It is also reasonable that Aki's son contemplates a career in politics as so many Japanese Americans were doing, including George Ariyoshi, who served as governor for over a dozen years in the 1970s and 1980s and for whom, it is joked in *The Life of the Land*, a special chicken dish might be named. It is also reasonable to have the family business fail as Hawai'i goes through its own cycles of boom and bust.

It is, I think, worth mentioning some of the historical developments we cannot infer from Sakamoto's plays. We do not learn, for example, of the intense and sometimes bloody labor battles and strikes that plagued Hawai'i in the 1920s and 1930s. We see nothing of the anticommunist witch hunts of the 1950s, or the civil rights and antiwar activities of the 1960s and 1970s, or the struggles to protect land and lifestyle rights in the 1970s, or the emergence of a powerful renaissance of Native Hawaiian cultural and political activism challenging the new status quo in the 1970s and 1980s. We have no idea, also, that there was evolving a myth of enormous proportion—that of the extraordinary exploits and significance of Japanese American GIs during World War II and the alleged control of the Islands by this ethnic group.[9] These issues have little direct relationship to the stories told in Sakamoto's trilogy but are important in understanding the Kamiya family's history.

Social Background

Some of the differences between the Hawai'i of 1929 and 1980 are real and stark. In 1929, there were perhaps 360,000 residents living in a territory of the United States who, although citizens if born in Hawai'i, still had a governor appointed by the president and who had no voting representation in Congress. There were nearly 140,000 Japanese Americans, comprising the single largest ethnic group by far—almost 40 percent of the total. This figure includes immigrant issei, to whom the United States government denied naturalization rights until 1952. More to the point, the majority were younger nisei, like Aki and Tosh, who comprised more than one-half of the children in school and who would eventually form a plurality at the polls.[10]

By 1980, there were nearly one million people living in Hawai'i, and the demography had changed considerably; the Japanese American population had grown to about 220,000, but it was now less than one-fourth of the total. In the intervening years, the percentages of Native Hawaiians, Filipinos, Caucasians, and "others" had increased, and there were loud mutterings about the arrogance of Japanese Americans who allegedly controlled Hawai'i, or at least its public sector.[11] One result has been more interest in the inner dynamics of this ethnic group. Some of the speculations, both academic and popular, have been extremely problematic in their use of simplistic and stereotypical notions of Japanese or Japanese American culture and values.

These plays are extremely valuable as real data against which to measure the cultural values commonly attributed to Japanese Americans. Japanese Americans share the problems of every other ethnic or racial group in the perpetual, intraethnic, and intergenerational guerrila war of defining, defending, and reinventing our culture and values. We all face these conflicts as times and contexts change. To make matters worse, like other minority groups, we who are Japanese Americans still find ourselves perimetered by stereotypes. One of the strongest is that of the "perpetual foreigner" and the inscrutable bearer of ancient, unchanging, traditions. In many accounts, generations of Japanese Americans purportedly hark back to a mythical Meiji-era set of hidebound shibboleths.

There is no denying that the Japanese immigrants who left their homeland during the Meiji period, 1868–1911, brought enormous amounts of cultural baggage with them. The immigrant Kamiyas were surely part of that context. For them, these values were real; some of them even continue to have a degree of salience for contemporary generations: *oyakōkō*, filial piety; *gaman*, patience or repression; *enryo*, restraint; *shikata ga nai*, fatalism. But there has been a tendency to cluster these particular values and project a group personality of passivity and conformity. Even a cursory reading of this trilogy will alert us to the dangers of attributing these values, in oversimplified, overgeneralized terms, to Japanese Americans as a group. And yet, scholars, journalists, and politicians insist that this is a homogeneous group set apart by these values, whether as a "model minority" viewed as a beacon for America's benighted minorities or as an overrated collection of arrogant overachievers.[12]

This unfortunate mindset extends from historical analysis to the social sciences and literary criticism as well. Perhaps the most noteworthy direct application is in education and mental health, where too many professionals rely on these notions of cultural values.[13] There are now many attempts to provide instruction in sensitive cross-cultural techniques. In counseling or psychotherapy, basing analysis and treatment of contemporary Japanese Americans on the assumption that they simply retain old-world values is especially problematic. For this malady, Sakamoto's plays are a crucial antidote.[14] He shows us that cultural values are important—not only for the ways in which they guide or circumscribe behavior but for the manifold opportunities to express deviance or resistance.

Sakamoto treats *oyakōkō*, for example, in a highly nuanced and complex fashion. His accounts of two generations of children who, in spite of respect for their parents, follow their own hearts in order to leave or return "home" are fascinating and real. In this, the Kamiyas resemble the Oyama family in Milton Murayama's novel *All I Asking for Is My Body* more than most textbook interpretations. Indeed, Sakamoto's treatment of the ways in which the Kamiya family inherits, alters, and redefines "Japanese" values is exceedingly important.

It may be assumed that language maintenance would be among the values most highly treasured among the immigrants. Yet, even here there is ample room for discussion. It is true that Japanese language schools were among the earliest and most important institutions established by the issei. But they were only partially successful in convincing the nisei that learning the language was of value. Some of the issei learned Hawaiian well enough to conduct commerce and work alongside native people. A number of the early dictionaries created for the immigrants were trilingual—English, Japanese, Hawaiian. Most telling, the rudimentary pidgin that served the issei in crude interactions with bosses or other immigrant workers evolved into the more sophisticated Hawaiian Creole English, which the nisei helped to fashion.

A native speaker of Pidgin English, Sakamoto crafts the language of his characters carefully and lovingly. What Hawai'i residents call "Pidgin" is indigenous to the Islands, a unique language of its own, one that has been studied for some decades now by a number of scholars.[15] Its continued use and development among local residents, especially the youth, are a source of embarassment and frustration for those who feel that it represents deviance from "standard" English or a manifestation of educational or cultural deficit. Widespread use of Pidgin, for many educators in particular, is perceived to be the result of negative attitudes toward schooling or sloppy language habits. On the other hand, Pidgin has evolved and developed for over a century and seems unlikely to disappear. This is especially true among local performers, who make good use of its considerable comedic potential. But there is now a significant movement to incorporate Pidgin in contemporary writings. Indeed, Sakamoto is in the front ranks of writers who legitimize its value for the general public by using it in authentic contexts rather than as humor or caricature. It is natural for Pidgin, then, to be included among the most important markers of a "local" identity. Newcomers who want to belong in circles that cross ethnicity, class, and generation must at least understand or appreciate this language, if not speak it proficiently.

Sakamoto is not unique in his use of Pidgin. Other writers have done so to good effect, including another Hawai'i playwright and short story writer, Darrell Lum. Murayama's novel *All I Asking for Is My Body*, with its liberal doses of Pidgin dialogue, has become a classic of a Japanese American family set in Maui in the 1930s.[16] His second novel, *Five Years on a Rock*, focuses on the immigrant generation of the Oyama family but includes enough Pidgin conversation among nisei to provide a sense of authenticity.[17] It seems to me that Sakamoto's use of Pidgin is unusual in its more demanding or even unrelenting quality. Where Murayama, for example, deliberately employs Pidgin sparingly to ensure that the general audience can follow, Sakamoto challenges and occasionally frustrates the audience. The printed page in a novel makes it possible to turn back to or place an unfamiliar term in context. The rapid tempo of Sakamoto's plays makes his Pidgin more difficult to follow. Because Pidgin is a living language, it has changed significantly over time and varies among ethnic groups and regions within Hawai'i. Thus, even among local audiences, some miss subtleties in Sakamoto's dialogues and find that parts of the conversation elude them. And because this is a Japanese American family, the conversations are laced with Japanese terms familiar, primarily, to Japanese Americans who have lived in some proximity to their immigrant roots.[18]

Indeed, critics have called for a glossary "of the many Japanese words and phrases scattered throughout the dialogue. Most [Hawai'i] residents probably know baka and shiishii, but why not give everyone who isn't fluent in Japanese the chance to learn?"[19] Many of these terms may be comprehended in context or as they are rephrased in standard English dialogue, but Sakamoto's language—his particular Japanese terms and his Pidgin—is situated in specific ethnohistorical context and, as a result, can use some lexical support. I have created a glossary, which is found following the plays. But note that it is fluency in "Hawaiian Japanese American" of the mid-twentieth century that is the issue, not fluency in Japanese *per se,* because the native Japanese person from Tokyo (or Kumamoto) would be hard pressed to understand Sakamoto.[20]

In *The Taste of Kona Coffee,* Aki explores the complexity and contradictions created as a result of tensions within the evolving use of Japanese values. Talking to Tosh about leaving Kona, Aki reveals his grudging respect for their father who must "sacrifice personal freedom fo' da good of da family. 'S right, you gotta do dat.... And Otōsan believe in dat. 'S why he love da Chūshingura story so much. W'en da forty-seven loyal samurai wen' give up deir own life to avenge deir Lord Asano fo' da honor of da clan. 'S da whole Japanee style go back hundreds and hundreds of years." But, critically, in the end Aki tells Tosh that the clash of values means "it's eidda Otōsan or us. And Otōsan gotta lose" (Act II, Scene 4). It is no coincidence that *Chushingura* is Sakamoto's favorite story, although it bears repeating that in his own plays the children (except for Daniel in *The Life of the Land*) are invariably successful when rebelling against their parents.[21]

Some of the most telling scenes are the ones in which Sakamoto establishes the conflict between the issei parents and the nisei sons. Aki assures Tosh that they must not lose heart in the battle to convince their parents to move to Honolulu. He says: "dis is like one war between Japan and America.... people who wen' come from Japan, dey get deir own ideas about how to live, ideas from Japan. I no blame dem. 'S how dey was raised. Dey dunno any betta. But us guys, eh, we born in Hawai'i. We American citizens, right?... Japan is da past." Tosh demurs: "da Japan way is strong," but Aki goes on, "Nemmine dat. No fo'get, we gotta win da war, we gotta win da war" (Act II, Scene 1).

It seems to me that Sakamoto is most direct in the last scene of *The*

Life of the Land, the last play of the trilogy. There is, he seems to say, a difficult reality to the power of the culture. Danny, the grandson of Aki, the original Kamiya rebel, is expected to go to Yale on the success track but has developed a strong attachment to Aki and the nursery. It is Aki, finally, who convinces Danny that he should follow his parents' wishes and go to college. Spencer, who had successfully defied his father in order to leave the family construction business, tells his young nephew, "Danny, it's not easy being Japanese."

In *The Life of the Land,* Debbie reinforces this feeling. Debbie is Spencer's younger sister, who is in conflict over a decision to leave Hawai'i. She sums up the frustration of family and individual conflicts with an anguished " 's what I hate about being Japanese. Too damn dopey about stupid things" (end of Act II, Scene 1). In the same play, we find that Spencer's older sister had taken responsibility for the family business and had been their father's confidante and support. Still, Laura reports that when she sat by her father as he lay dying, "all he said was 'Spenca, come help me. Spenca.' I guess he was still thinking of you at the end" (Act II, Scene 2).

The centrality of the oldest son, the *chōnan,* is one of the more powerful values in Japanese culture. It is a role full of privilege and responsibility, of potential for mischief and abuse. Aki, the *chōnan* of the immigrant Kamiyas, reflects this in his anguish over the responsibility he must shoulder and in his revelation that there was an older son who had died twenty years earlier: "Too bad he wen ma-ke. . . . Kishiyo, why you wen' die fo' " (*The Taste of Kona Coffee,* Act II, Scene 4). An older brother would have removed much of the burden from Aki's own shoulders even as it would have deprived him of the perquisites of status. Milton Murayama also explores this theme in *Five Years on a Rock* and provides telling evidence of the eldest son finding himself in a difficult position.[22]

In situations where resources were extremely limited, it probably made sense, practically as well as culturally, to concentrate family energies in the future of the *chōnan.* Where group mobility was difficult, one of the few ways to create more opportunity for an entire family was to focus on the fortunes of an individual. This was fairly typical of cultures in which upward mobility was both sought and restricted. This combination of expectations simultaneously established more pressure to conform and more freedom for individualistic behavior on the part of the eldest son.

Another intensely personal theme is that of "moving on" and "going home," which runs through the trilogy. *The Taste of Kona Coffee* has Aki, the older son, leaving Kona first but returning to rescue his brother, Tosh, from the stifling context of rural coffee farming. Almost parenthetically, Sakamoto describes the desperate attempts of a young neighbor who attempts to seduce Aki as a way of escaping Kona.[23] In *Mānoa Valley*, Tosh discovers that his son, Spencer, rejects the comfortable life planned for him and must leave Hawai'i for school on the mainland. Finally, in *The Life of the Land*, twenty years after leaving Hawai'i, Spencer determines that he must go home again.

The Playwright

Sakamoto is sometimes asked how his own life has been reconciled with these tensions. When mainlanders ask how he could have left such a wonderful place, Sakamoto responds, "I had to. Hawai'i seemed too small for a youthful dreamer. You have to go to the mainland to better yourself, to get opportunities unavailable [in Hawai'i]. . . . Now that I'm fifty-three, with a steady job and lifestyle and settled in Los Angeles, I'm beginning to wonder. Should I have stayed in Hawai'i? It's almost impossible to come back without tremendous sacrifice. A decision in my youth has led to serious consequences in my middle age. I never foresaw that."[24] Sakamoto has considered a return to Hawai'i although the financial constraints have always made it difficult. At one point, he reflected on the fate of Hawai'i "exiles" who "are in limbo. . . . We don't belong on the mainland and we don't belong in Hawai'i anymore, . . . I don't necessarily feel that the mainland is my home. Honolulu will always be my home."[25]

He is considering whether this is the time for serious planning; he knows full well that the cost of living, especially housing, is a major obstacle. So is the availability of appropriate employment. But he senses that time is running short, and conditions in the Los Angeles area continue to deteriorate, so he is "determined" to make a real effort to return to Hawai'i.[26]

Ed Sakamoto has been a copy editor for the *Los Angeles Times* for nearly two decades and pursues his play-writing career from his home in Monterey Park. His plays are not strictly autobiographical; unlike Aki and Tosh, he was reared in 'A'ala Park in Honolulu, for example. But both his parents were from Kona on the Big Island and he recalls that his mother, especially, often told him stories of their early years there.[27] His interest in writing began in the ninth grade as a student at 'Iolani School.[28] For extra credit, Sakamoto rewrote the last third of Robert Louis Stevenson's *Trea-*

sure Island because he did not particularly like the ending. His teacher, Thomas Raney, was enthusiastic, said he liked Sakamoto's version better than Stevenson's, and read the whole section to the class. Young Edward was hooked for life.

In his junior year, Sakamoto's speech and drama teacher, Dorothy Matsinger, cast him in a costarring role in the play *On the Night of January 16th*. The next year, she had him play the lead, Thomas Beckett, in T. S. Eliot's *Murder in the Cathedral*. But, as Sakamoto later noted, "I'm glad I never pursued acting. For one thing, I wouldn't have been that good. Plus I don't like the nomadic lifestyle, the constant auditioning and rejection I see Asian American actors go through. It's pathetic the kinds of roles they play in TV and the movies. . . . I suppose one reason I began writing Asian American plays is that we lacked plays where Asian Americans are the 'stars,' where the central characters were us and not them, and the stories revolved around us."

In the Alley was Sakamoto's first play. Sakamoto wrote it in a playwriting class taught by Edward Langhans. He was in his junior year at the University of Hawai'i.[29] The play won a campus prize and was produced at the university. Sakamoto recalls how exhilarating it was to sit in the audience and hear the positive response. But this was to be the high point of his writing in Hawai'i. "I was never able to write another play in Hawai'i. Theater back then was nothing more than . . . Broadway shows and . . . summer stock plays like *Under the Yum Yum Tree*. Nothing much there for an Asian American playwright." Dennis Carroll considers *In the Alley* "the best short play ever written in Hawai'i on the dynamics of racial conflict."[30]

Sakamoto graduated from the University of Hawai'i in 1962 and moved to the mainland in 1966. He did not write another play until 1972, while living in southern California. He submitted it to an East West Players' contest; it did not win, but the artistic director, Mako, staged *Yellow Is My Favorite Color*. Mako, the veteran actor once nominated for an Academy Award for best supporting actor in *Sand Pebbles*, has been a key figure in Asian American theater and film.[31] For Sakamoto, Mako was a "big influence in that he staged so many of my plays in the '70s and '80s. The experience of writing plays and having them staged so quickly so often was invaluable, something I wish all playwrights could have."

Of course, there was always some ambivalence: "The negative side, if one would call it that, is I never made contact with mainstream 'white' theaters and cultivated an association with them." But this was something of a mixed blessing: "Who knows how warped my writing would have become if I had constantly worked with white dramaturges and artistic directors who have their own view as to what plays should say or do." Thus, working with East West Players in Los Angeles, Pan Asian Repertory in New York City, and Kumu Kahua in Honolulu "was more beneficial in the long run."[32]

Sakamoto had a deeply moving experience after the curtain fell on the first performance of *Mānoa Valley* by the East West Players in Los Angeles. An Asian American male approached him to exclaim that there was an instant shock of recognition when nisei Tosh appeared on stage at the beginning of the play. "When the character came out in his underwear, I said, 'That's my brother.'" Sakamoto realized that this man, perhaps for the first time, was seeing an actor on stage "he could identify with as someone from his own world and not the white man's world. It made an impression on me. And I thought Asian Americans should be able to see themselves portrayed on stage—to show that they are as important as whites and that their stories deserved to be told too."[33]

The opportunity to work with Mako and the East West Players was critical for Sakamoto. Play after play was performed, and Sakamoto was recognized with two Hollywood Drama-Logue Critic Awards for Outstanding Achievement in Writing for *Chikamatsu's Forest* and *Stew Rice*. He received grants from the National Endowment for the Arts and Rockefeller Foundation, including the prestigious Rockefeller Foundation American Playwrights in Residence Award for work with the East West Players in 1980–1981. The county of Los Angeles issued a proclamation commending his contributions. In Hawai'i, Sakamoto received the Po'okela Award for *Aloha Las Vegas* for Excellence in Original Script in 1993.

Coming home for Ed Sakamoto, the playwright, would involve confronting ethnic and racial contexts vastly different from those he now faces in Los Angeles. "Home" is, moreover, always problematic after any lengthy sojourn; family relationships change, neighborhoods develop, friends evolve, we ourselves are transformed; we speak differently, even if we deliberately avoid the pretensions of the Kamiya neighbor who had gone to the mainland for college in *The Taste of Kona Coffee*.

In this increasingly diverse and multicultural world, we need the widest possible variety of venues through which we may understand one another.[34] Theater has always been one of the most effective means of intercultural communication, and Ed Sakamoto's trilogy dealing with the Kamiya family articulates one important set of Japanese American experiences. These plays will, I am sure, provide much pleasure and information and encourage even more writing and production.

NOTES

1. For a good introduction to local theater in Hawai'i, see Dennis Carroll, "Introduction," in *Kumu Kahua Plays*, ed. Dennis Carroll (Honolulu: University of Hawai'i Press, 1983).

2. David Henry Hwang, Velina Hasu Houston, Frank Chin, Wakako Yamauchi, and Philip Kan Gotanda are among the playwrights who have had their works produced in many regional theaters and on Broadway.

3. Franklin Odo and Kazuko Sinoto, *A Pictorial History of the Japanese in Hawai'i, 1885–1924* (Honolulu: Bishop Museum Press, 1985), pp. 121–125.

4. Any cursory review of letters to the daily newspapers in Honolulu over a period of some months would reveal the degree of dissatisfaction with the ethnic group and the party. For a more analytical view, see George Cooper and Gavan Daws, *Land and Power in Hawaii: The Democratic Years* (Honolulu: University of Hawai'i Press, 1985).

5. Noel Kent, *Hawaii: Islands Under the Influence* (Honolulu: University of Hawai'i Press, 1993), p. 83.

6. Ibid.

7. For a brief overview of this process, see Roland Kotani, *The Japanese in Hawaii: A Century of Struggle* (Honolulu: Hawai'i Hochi, 1985), pp. 73–127.

8. Kent, p. 121.

9. There is a vast literature and set of documentaries on the World War II veterans. Among the most noteworthy: Masayo Duus, *Unlikely Liberators: The Men of the 100th and 442nd* (Honolulu: University of Hawai'i Press, 1987); Chester Tanaka, *Go For Broke: A Pictorial History of the Japanese American 100th Infantry Battalion and the 442nd Regimental Combat Team* (San Francisco: Go For Broke, Inc., 1982); John Tsukano, *Bridge of Love* (Honolulu: Hawaii Hosts, Inc., 1985); Thelma Chang, *I Can Never Forget* (Honolulu: Sigi Productions, 1991). For an extended treatment of one group of nisei, the Varsity Victory Volunteers, see Franklin Odo, *No Sword to Bury, No Flag to Burn*, forthcoming.

10. A detailed treatment of the nisei in the pre–World War II period is in Eileen Tamura's *Americanization, Assimilation and Ethnic Identity: The Nisei Generation in Hawaii* (Urbana and Chicago: University of Illinois Press, 1994).

11. For population shifts, see the convenient tables in Eleanor Nordyke, *The Peopling of Hawai'i* (Honolulu: University of Hawai'i Press, 1989), pp. 173–265.

12. See, for example, the collection of essays in *The State of Asian Pacific America: Policy Issues to the Year 2020* (Los Angeles: LEAP Asian Pacific American Public Policy Institute and UCLA Asian American Studies Center, 1993). For a brief overview of the model minority thesis including an effective critique, see Sucheng Chan, *Asian Americans: An Interpretive History* (Boston: Twayne, 1991), pp. 167–185.

13. The essays on "Education K–12 Policy" by Peter Kiang and Vivian Lee and on "Mental Health Policy" by Stanley Sue in *Policy Issues to the Year 2020* are instructive.

14. There is a long tradition of such representation. It is possible to understand the works of writers such as Bill Hosokawa (*Nisei: The Quiet Americans* [New York: Wm Morrow, 1969]) or Harry Kitano (*Japanese Americans: The Evolution of a Subculture*

[Englewood Cliffs, N.J.: Prentice-Hall, 1969]), who after all were reared in a community dominated by issei who tried to maintain traditional cultural values, albeit in attenuated form. It is more difficult to understand sansei who perpetuate these notions in spite of considerable behavioral evidence to the contrary (see, for example, Dennis Ogawa, *Kodomo no Tame ni: For the Sake of the Children* [Honolulu: University Press of Hawai'i, 1978]). It is quite remarkable to find contemporary expression of this notion in academic journals (Anthony Marsella, "Counseling and Psychotherapy with Japanese Americans: Cross-Cultural Considerations," *American Journal of Orthopsychiatry* 63(2) [April 1993]). Marsella's article has good advice for counselors and psychotherapists: "pursue knowledge of the Japanese-American experience as a way of enhancing the opportunity for therapeutic success" (p. 207). But the article assumes that even third and fourth generations of Japanese Americans are imbued with values, some of which may be traced for hundreds or thousands of years, and which have "resulted in a highly homogeneous culture"—in itself a highly questionable assertion, given the regional, linguistic, and cultural variations among Japanese of Ainu, *buraku*, Korean, and Okinawan descent, to mention just the most obvious; in addition, historical context, age, religion, region, gender, and class have always been critical boundaries and borders. To suggest that the highly inflammatory *yamato damashi*, for an extreme example, is still important is strange; it is not merely, as Marsella suggests, "a belief in Japanese ascendancy," but is an expression of extreme chauvinism used to justify the imperial and colonial horrors perpetrated on the rest of Asia in the 1930s and 1940s. The nisei were especially sensitive to this issue since racism linked them culturally and politically to their parents' homelands and because many were aware of atrocities being committed by the Japanese in Asia. While international relations do not figure in his plays, Sakamoto is clear about the contest within the household between old and new. For a more reasoned account of understanding and utilizing Japanese cultural values in therapy, see Betty S. Furuta, "Ethnic Identities of Japanese-American Families: Implications for Counseling," in *Understanding the Family: Stress and Change in American Family Life*, ed. Cathleen Getty and Winnifred Humphreys (New York: Appleton-Century-Crofts, 1981).

15. See especially Charlene Sato's important works that build upon the pioneering efforts of earlier scholars such as John Reinecke and Stanley Tsuzaki. Sato, "Linguistic Inequality in Hawai'i: The Post-Creole Dilemma," in *Language of Inequality*, ed. Nessa Wolfson and Joan Manes (Berlin: Mouton, 1985); and "Sociolinguistic Variation and Language Attitudes in Hawai'i," in *English around the World: Sociolinguistic Perspectives*, ed. Jenny Cheshire (Cambridge: Cambridge University Press, 1991). Also, see Carol Odo's pioneering technical analysis in her unpublished Ph.D. dissertation, "Phonological Processes in the English Dialect of Hawaii," University of Hawai'i at Mānoa, 1975. See also her pronunciation guide in *Kumu Kahua Plays*, pp. 239–245.

16. Stephen Sumida locates the first use of Pidgin for more than "merely comic effect" in 1936 with University of Hawai'i students in a drama-writing class. "Waiting for the Big Fish: Recent Research in the Asian American Literature of Hawaii," in *The Best of Bamboo Ridge*, ed. Eric Chock and Darrell H. Y. Lum (Honolulu: Bamboo Ridge Press, 1986), p. 312. Milton Murayama's three-part novella was first published in 1975; it has since been reprinted many times, most recently by the University of Hawai'i Press in 1988. For a brief discussion of Murayama's use of Pidgin, see my Afterword,

"The Hawaii Nisei: Tough Talk and Sweet Sugar," in *All I Asking for Is My Body* (Honolulu: University of Hawai'i, 1988), pp. 105–110. Sumida takes special note of Philip Ige's earlier short story, "The Forgotten Flea Powder," which was published in *Paradise of the Pacific* 58 (November 1946): 24–25 and reprinted in *Bamboo Ridge: The Hawaii Writers' Quarterly* 1 (December 1978): 56–59.

17. Honolulu: University of Hawai'i Press, 1994.

18. Sakamoto's Japanese terms are directly from his mother's stories. He does not know Japanese well but believes that some of them are regional dialect, from her Kumamoto background. Personal communication, January 14, 1994.

19. John Berger, "Stage Review: Company Brews Fine 'Coffee'," *Honolulu Star-Bulletin*, September 22, 1993.

20. It is interesting to note, however, that both *Mānoa Valley* and *The Life Of The Land* were performed by the Pan Asian Repertory Theater in New York City. Sakamoto was not able to see for himself but was told that the audiences were able to follow and appreciate the language. It was a happy circumstance that several fine actors from Hawai'i, including Kati Kuroda, were with that group. Personal communication, January 14, 1994.

21. Sakamoto wrote a play, *Chikamatsu's Forest*, about Chikamatsu Monzaemon, who wrote the most famous of the works dealing with this famous story. Interview by Mike Gordon, *Honolulu Star-Bulletin*, May 5, 1988, pp. B1, 6.

22. Murayama's protagonist is Sawa Oyama, who arrived in Hawai'i as a picture bride, married to a cousin, Isao. The family relationships are extremely strained and she is even forced to sympathize with Isao, whose father seems to depend on him for work while excusing the other two boys. "Isao had inherited all the disadvantages but none of the advantages of a number one son" (p. 61).

23. For the best description of the desperate lives of Kona's coffee farmers in the 1920s and 1930s, see Koji Ariyoshi's moving account of his family during that period. Ariyoshi wrote a series of articles for the *Honolulu Record*, the newspaper he edited for the ILWU, in the mid-1950s while being persecuted and prosecuted for left-wing beliefs. He titled the articles "My Thoughts for which I Stand Indicted" and effectively used the forum to articulate a progressive interpretation of Hawai'i's history as well as the injustices of the McCarthy-period witch hunts in the Islands. Kotani, pp. 120–127.

24. Burl Burlingame, "A Taste of Ed Sakamoto," *Honolulu Star-Bulletin*, September 15, 1993, pp. B1, 4.

25. Ibid.

26. Personal communication, January 14, 1994.

27. Ibid.

28. Mr. Sakamoto kindly agreed to provide me with personal details for this essay. This section is largely based on his letter. Sakamoto to Odo, December 30, 1993.

29. Sakamoto to Odo, December 21, 1993. I am deeply grateful to Sakamoto for responding so quickly and positively to requests for information.

30. Dennis Carroll, p. 123.

31. See especially Yumiko Murakami, "Isuto mitsu uesto: Mako to Suji no Nichibei monogatari" (East meets West: the Japan-America tale of Mako and Suzi) (Tokyo: Kodansha, 1993).

32. Sakamoto to Odo, December 21, 1993.
33. Sakamoto to Odo, December 30, 1993.
34. For a good introduction to the realm of Asian Americans within this context, see *The State of Asian Pacific America: Policy Issues to the Year 2020* (Los Angeles: LEAP Asian Pacific American Policy Institute and UCLA Asian American Studies Center, 1993).

Acknowledgments

I AM FOREVER INDEBTED to Dr. Dennis Carroll of the University of Hawai'i theater department, who as managing director of Kumu Kahua urged me to write the third play of the trilogy. His enthusiasm and support encouraged me as I worked to complete *The Taste of Kona Coffee*. Dr. Carroll then produced the trilogy in an exciting and ambitious program at Kumu Kahua, an event I will always cherish. My thanks also to Mako, who staged nine of my plays when he was artistic director at East West Players in Los Angeles, premiering *Mānoa Valley* and *The Life of the Land*. To Dr. Glenn Cannon, my gratitude for staging *Mānoa Valley* at the University of Hawai'i's Kennedy Theatre. And, finally, kudos to the actors, technical artists, and directors for taking my characters on the printed page and making them come alive on stage.

Production Credits

THE TRILOGY was first presented in integral performances by Kumu Kahua Theatre for a season in its new premises in the restored Kamehameha V Post Office, 46 Merchant Street, Honolulu, for four weekend performances beginning February 26, 1994. Total playing time, with forty-five-minute intermissions between the plays, was six and a half hours. The plays had earlier been offered in separate productions with identical casts, directors, and designers to those listed below. *The Taste of Kona Coffee* opened for ten performances at Tenney Theatre, St. Andrew's Cathedral, beginning September 17, 1993; *Mānoa Valley* for ten performances at Tenney Theatre, beginning November 26, 1993; and *The Life of the Land* opened at Kumu Kahua Theatre, February 11, 1994. The latter production played concurrently with that of the complete trilogy.

THE TASTE OF KONA COFFEE

CAST

MIKAME KAMIYA Karen Yamamoto Hackler
KAZUO KAMIYA Dann Seki
TOSHIO (TOSH) KAMIYA Devon M. T. Nekoba
AKIRA (AKI) KAMIYA Marcus R. Oshiro
SHOGO Michael W. Lee
TOMI ISHITANI Michelle Sekine
HARUKO ISHITANI Amy M. Nishihara
JIRO SAKAI Michael W. Lee

Directed by James A. Nakamoto

MĀNOA VALLEY

CAST

TOSH KAMIYA Devon M. T. Nekoba
FUMIKO KAMIYA Nyla L. Fujii
DEBBIE KAMIYA Michelle A. Kim
SPENCER KAMIYA Michael W. Lee
LAURA KAMIYA TANIGUCHI Marya A. Takamori
AKI KAMIYA Marcus R. Oshiro
NOBU KAMIYA Dann Seki
SUSAN KAMIYA Justina T. Mattos
TOMI KAMIYA Jan M. K. Kanaeholo
TOKU TANIGUCHI Rodney Kwock

Directed by Keith Kashiwada

THE LIFE OF THE LAND

CAST

LAURA KAMIYA TANIGUCHI Marya A. Takamori
DEBBIE KAMIYA Michelle A. Kim
TOKU TANIGUCHI Rodney Kwock
SPENCER KAMIYA Michael W. Lee
MAXWELL LAM Justin Kuwamura
AKI KAMIYA Marcus R. Oshiro
DANIEL KAMIYA Devon M. T. Nekoba
FUMIKO KAMIYA Nyla L. Fujii
NOBU KAMIYA Dann Seki
SUSAN KAMIYA Justina T. Mattos

Directed by John H. Y. Wat

FOR THE TRILOGY

HAWAI'I NO KA OI

Associate Director Harry Wong III
Set Design by Joseph D. Dodd
Lighting Design by Gerald Kawaoka
Costume design by Linda Yara
Makeup and Wig Design by Newton K. Koshi
Sound and Music Design by Keith Kashiwada
Kumu Kahua Theatre Artistic Director: Gene Shofner
Kumu Kahua Theatre Managing Director: Dennis Carroll

The full-length version of *Mānoa Valley* was first produced by the Department of Theatre and Dance, University of Hawai'i at Mānoa, at Kennedy Theatre, Honolulu, for a season beginning April 2, 1982.

CAST

TOSH KAMIYA Stanford Egi
FUMIKO KAMIYA Cynthia See
LAURA KAMIYA Suzanne Park
SPENCER KAMIYA Clyde Yasuhara
DEBBIE KAMIYA Alison Uyeda
UNCLE AKI Gary N. Nomura
AUNTIE TOMI Kati Kuroda
NOBU Darryl Tsutsui
SUSAN Emily Dorsett
TOKU Mitchell Young

Directed by Glenn Cannon
Scene Design by Wayne Higa
Lighting and Technical Direction by Mark Boyd
Costume Design by JanDee Abraham
Incidental Music Composed and Arranged by Allen Trubitt

A different version of *The Life of the Land* was premiered at East West Players in Los Angeles in July 1981. This version was first presented by Kumu Kahua at Kawaiahao Hall, Mid-Pacific Institute, Honolulu, for a season beginning March 8, 1985.

CAST

DEBBIE KAMIYA Suzanne Park
LAURA TANIGUCHI Kat Yashiki
TOKU TANIGUCHI Rodney Chang
SPENCER KAMIYA Gary Nomura
MAXWELL LAM Leighton Liu
AKI KAMIYA Ben H. Tamashiro
DANIEL KAMIYA John Kamada
FUMIKO KAMIYA Gloria Tamashiro
NOBU KAMIYA Dennis Chun
SUSAN KAMIYA Victoria N. Kneubuhl

Directed and Designed by Dando Kluever
Lighting Design by Donald R. Ranney, Jr.

THE TASTE OF KONA COFFEE

THE TASTE OF KONA COFFEE

Time: Summer of 1929.

Place: The Kamiya coffee farm in Kona, Hawai'i.

Scenery: The house sits at stage right. It is built with natural, unpainted wood. The roof is corrugated metal. A spacious porch has places for shoes and slippers. There is a wooden rocking chair and a small round table and a stool. Hoes and other farm tools are situated at the side of the house.

CHARACTERS

KAZUO KAMIYA, *head of the household, in his mid-sixties*
MIKAME KAMIYA, *kazuo's wife, in her fifties*
TOSHIO (TOSH) KAMIYA, *son, age twenty*
AKIRA (AKI) KAMIYA, *son, twenty-five*
SHOGO, *farm worker, twenty*
TOMIKO (TOMI) ISHITANI, *family helper, twenty-three*
HARUKO ISHITANI, *TOMI's sister, eighteen*
JIRO SAKAI, *neighbor, twenty-one (Same actor plays Shogo and Jiro)*

ACT ONE
Scene 1

(*A bright and sunny morning. Birds chirp occasionally.* MIKAME *comes out and holds the door open. Out steps* TOSH *as he helps* KAZUO, *who can barely walk, to the rocking chair.* MIKAME *stirs up a soapy mixture in a cup and puts lather on* KAZUO's *face. Then she expertly strops a hand razor over a leather strap.* TOSH *sits on the porch, looking offstage as if he's expecting someone.* MIKAME *begins shaving* KAZUO.)

TOSH: Nice day today. . . . Special day.

MIKAME: Why special?

KAZUO: Hoe hana day.

TOSH: No, not that.

KAZUO: Today work, every day work. Nothing special. . . . Where Shogo?

TOSH: Not here yet.

KAZUO: I have to scold him. Always late. Just like his father. Good for nothing.
(MIKAME *pulls back his head to shave at the neck.*)
Oi, watch out. My head is not a coconut.

MIKAME: Sorry.

KAZUO: I have to check the trees on the north side when Shogo comes. I hope there's no disease.

MIKAME: If the trees and leaves turn black, we might lose the whole coffee crop again.

TOSH: No, I checked. The trees are fine. I don't think it'll happen again. That thing before, it was a real mystery.

KAZUO: There are things I want Shogo to do. I have to show him everything or he just stands around scratching his head.

TOSH: I can tell him what to do.

KAZUO: No, have to be me.

TOSH: You can hardly walk, Otōsan. I'll take him.

KAZUO: No, no, I can. My legs will get stronger. Wait and see.

TOSH: Sadamu Kunimoto left for Honolulu yesterday.

MIKAME: So he finally went.

KAZUO: That Sadamu was always lazy. I feel sorry for the Kunimotos. Sadamu will turn out bad, run around with the wrong people. Nothing but trouble.

MIKAME: His mother is so worried. He'll be alone in Honolulu. The city is too big.
TOSH: Aki's doing okay.
KAZUO: Sadamu is just like your brother.
(SHOGO *enters. He wears work clothes and a dirty, battered baseball cap.*)
SHOGO: Here I am. Sorry I'm a little late. I was cleaning up Mr. Cameron's yard.
MIKAME: You have too many jobs, Shogo.
SHOGO: Well, I don't need too much sleep, so I have more time for work. That's good.
KAZUO: But if you come here late, that's not good.
SHOGO: Sorry. I will remember that the next time. I'll get up a little earlier. Then I can get here sooner from Mr. Cameron's.
KAZUO: Shogo, help me. I have to show you what to do on the north side. Hayō, hayō.
MIKAME: Your face first.
KAZUO: Never mind my face. No time now.
(*He leans heavily on* SHOGO *and they start off.* TOSH *tries to help;* KAZUO *waves him away.*)
Don't bother, don't bother.
(KAZUO *and* SHOGO *struggle off.*)
MIKAME: Don't forget you have to see the doctor after lunch.
TOSH: Otōsan is so stubborn.
MIKAME: Come, I'll cut your hair now.
TOSH: It's not too long.
MIKAME: I have everything here.
TOSH: Today is a special day . . . because Aki is coming home—on the *Humuʻula*.
MIKAME: Akira? Why?
TOSH: I asked him to.
MIKAME: And he said okay? Okashii. Something wrong with him? Did police arrest him or something?
TOSH: No, nothing like that. I thought he should come home once in a while.
MIKAME: Hmmm, I wonder how he looks now.
TOSH: Funny. He asked how you looked, too.
MIKAME: I haven't changed much in six years.
TOSH: You still look so young, Okāsan.
MIKAME: Is he homesick? Maybe he wants to come home for good.

TOSH: No, just to visit. He said he can stay for a week only.
MIKAME: Why only a week?
TOSH: He's busy. . . . Okāsan, would you like to visit Honolulu?
MIKAME: I was there already. When I first came to Hawai'i as a picture bride, I saw all I needed of that place.
TOSH: I still haven't seen Honolulu.
MIKAME: You haven't missed anything.
TOSH: Okāsan, I want to go there.
MIKAME: Someday. Maybe next year, after we finish picking the coffee.
TOSH: No, I mean I want to go to Honolulu to live.
MIKAME: What?
TOSH: To go to school. Okāsan, I want to study there. I want to learn to build houses and be my own boss. I want to build nice homes for people to live in. Make them my way.
MIKAME: You can't do that.
TOSH: Why not?
MIKAME: That's for haoles to do.
TOSH: No, not just haoles.
MIKAME: Haoles have money and go to the university to learn. You can't be the same as them.
TOSH: I know I only have a sixth-grade education, but still I don't want to be a farmer all my life.
MIKAME: I'm sorry you couldn't continue with school, but we needed you on the farm.
TOSH: I know. Aki too. I know.
MIKAME: But we are a family of farmers. Otōsan's father, his father, and his father. That was my life in Kumamoto, too. My father and his father and his father. It's a hard life, but it's our life. That's all we know.
TOSH: That's why I want to study to be something else. So I don't have to be a farmer. And I don't want my son to be a farmer either.
MIKAME: You want to be like Aki. Run away to Honolulu and leave Otōsan and me.
TOSH: No, I would never do that. I won't leave you. I want you and Otōsan to come too.
MIKAME: To Honolulu? What would Otōsan do?
TOSH: He wouldn't have to do a thing. He can hardly walk anyway. He's useless. I'll take care of you and Otōsan. I'll go to work someplace and go to school at night.
MIKAME: Otōsan won't go.

TOSH: He has to. That's why I asked Aki to come and talk to him.
MIKAME: Baka. You think Otōsan is going to listen to Aki?
TOSH: Well, I know Otōsan won't listen to me. I thought maybe Aki might—
MIKAME: Otōsan's whole life is in Kona. This farm. He loves this place. He would rather die than move from here.
TOSH: Don't say that, please.
MIKAME: Can't you be happy here? You're not like Aki. You're sensible, hard working, serious.
TOSH: Yes, I am different from Aki. You know I won't go to Honolulu just to play. I want to improve myself.
MIKAME: Then try to be the best farmer in Kona.
TOSH: Okāsan, I have nothing against farmers, but I have my own dreams. Is it fair to me? Should I stay a farmer, just to make Otōsan happy?
MIKAME: What about me? Don't you want to make me happy?
TOSH: Okāsan, most of all I want you to be happy. I want to buy things for you. A nice, big house. New clothes. All the modern things they have in Honolulu. I want the people in Kona to be jealous. You can show off all your new possessions.
MIKAME: I'm your mother, but you don't know me. After all these years, you don't know me. I'm a country person. I don't need or want those things. I'm happy here. . . . You have to take Otōsan to Doctor Hayashi. Otōsan had a hard life and now this is his reward.
(*Lights fade to black.*)

Scene 2

(*Later in the afternoon.* AKI *enters, carrying a beat-up travel bag. He looks around, remembering, then sits on the ground.* MIKAME *comes out of the house, her back to* AKI. *She tidies up the porch as* AKI *watches.*)

AKI: Okāsan.
MIKAME: Akira.
   (*He walks over and embraces her. She doesn't put her arms around him.*)
AKI: Okāsan.
MIKAME: What?
AKI: Good to see you.
MIKAME: You lost weight.

AKI: The cafes I go to, they don't know how to cook like you.
MIKAME: We have leftover nishime. Go inside and eat.
AKI: Let me stay out here a while. Otōsan in the house?
MIKAME: Toshio took him to the doctor.
AKI: Oh, good.
MIKAME: How are your ears?
AKI: My ears? Daijōbu. My ears are so sharp I can even hear cockroaches talking to each other.
MIKAME: Come. Let me see.
AKI: I guess my ears could stand some cleaning.
(*He lies next to her on the edge of the porch and puts his head on her lap. She takes out a bobby pin from her hair and carefully digs into his ear.*) You haven't done this for me in a long time, Okāsan. Aahh, good, yeah, yeah, aahh.
MIKAME: Maaa, look at the mimi-kuso.
(*She puts the earwax in Aki's outstretched palm.*)
AKI: Hmmm, I guess my ears are all plugged up. People must be talking bad about me.
MIKAME: So what are you doing now?
AKI: Hmmm, I was driving a taxi for a time, driving a lot of soldiers back to Schofield Barracks. You know that Schofield place is big, lots of soldiers. I almost was going to join the Army one time when I was hungry, but then I thought, no, too many haoles in the Army, so instead I worked in a movie theater as a janitor. Aeehh, Okāsan, don't poke my ear.
MIKAME: Sorry. So, you went to Honolulu to become a janitor?
AKI: Only for a short time.
MIKAME: Let me see the other ear.
(*He moves over to the other side.*) So, working as a janitor is better than working as a coffee farmer?
AKI: No. Sweeping up everybody's mess, cleaning the toilets, all that made me very humble. But now I'm working in a nursery, helping Nakamura-san with plants. I guess some of the things Otōsan taught me helped. Nakamura-san likes my work. Sometimes we get drunk together. Aeehh, Okāsan, watch out how you dig in my ear.
MIKAME: Sorry. So, how drunk do you get?
AKI: Oh, not that much. Nakamura-san is the one who likes to drink, to relax after all the hard work in the hot sun. Nakamura-san is like a father to me. He says he's going to leave the nursery to me when he dies.

MIKAME: What about his family? No sons?
AKI: He left his wife in Japan. And she died in childbirth. The baby died too. That was a long time ago. So he's all alone.
MIKAME: You don't need his nursery. You have a coffee farm here.
AKI: The nursery is a good business. A lot of haoles give their business to Nakamura-san. He's very smart the way he talks to them.
MIKAME: Finish.
AKI: Feels good, Okāsan, dōmo arigatō.
MIKAME: Dō itashimashite. So, why did you come home?
AKI: Toshio didn't say?
MIKAME: You tell me.
AKI: Toshio wrote that Otōsan is real sick. He can't even walk without help. What's he going to do in September when it's time to pick the coffee?
MIKAME: He'll be better by then. Everything will be all right.
AKI: I hope so, for your sake. Otōsan is very demanding. Toshio said it's real hard on you.
MIKAME: It's a wife's duty to take care of her husband when he's sick. It's no hardship.
AKI: When I get married, I hope I find a wife just like you, Okāsan. Time for me to get married, I think.
MIKAME: What about the women in Honolulu? No good ones?
AKI: Not good like you, Okāsan. You know there's an American song that's very popular. (*Sings.*) I want a girl just like the girl that married dear old Dad. Understand?
MIKAME: Just find a Japanese wife who's not afraid of hard work.
(SHOGO *enters with a hoe.*)
Shogo, hungry now?
SHOGO: Hai, thank you, I could eat something.
AKI: Aeh, Shogo, 's you?
SHOGO: (*Looks at himself.*) Yeah.
AKI: Aeh, you no recognize me?
SHOGO: Ah, ah, wait. You not Aki, eh?
AKI: Of course, wat you tink? Only get one Aki.
SHOGO: Ooohh, Aki. Good you wen' come home. Long time I no see you. Boy, I wen' fo'get how you look.
AKI: You, too, Shogo. You sure wen' grow.
SHOGO: Yeah, well, I no can stay one kid all my life, eh.
MIKAME: I'll warm up some nishime for both of you.
(*She enters the house.*)

SHOGO: Aki, you wen' come back to live here?
AKI: No, jus' to visit. How's you muddah?
SHOGO: Oh, she wen' die four years ago.
AKI: Sorry, I neva hear dat.
SHOGO: 'S okay. Jus' me, myself now, nobody else.
AKI: Too bad.
SHOGO: Aki, you happy in Honolulu?
AKI: Yeah. Can't beat it. Lotta people, lotta tings fo' do, lotta wahines.
SHOGO: You get plenny girlfriends?
AKI: Oh yeah. Da girls ova dere, not like Kona girls.
SHOGO: Dey diff'rent?
AKI: Yeah, dey wear lipstick, nice dresses, perfume, and dey make da hair real fancy.
SHOGO: Even da Japanee girls?
AKI: Especially da Japanee girls.
SHOGO: No.
AKI: Aeh, I no kid you. And dey smell so good, like pīkake afta one light morning rain. You know, someday you gotta live in Honolulu.
SHOGO: Me? Nah. I no going leave dis island. But, Aki, good you wen' come back visit. I like show you someting.
AKI: Wat?
SHOGO: One obake.
AKI: Obake? Wat kine obake?
SHOGO: One lady ghost. She stay right here on dis property.
AKI: Our farm, here?
SHOGO: Yeah. I wen' tell your folks and Tosh, but dey no believe me.
AKI: And dis obake, she talk to you?
SHOGO: No, 's da ting. I can see her in da distance, but wen I go toward her, she run away. But I tell you, I see her.
AKI: Wen? At night?
SHOGO: Oh yeah, only at night. All dark and quiet, and she jus' standing dere by one mango tree.
AKI: Wich mango tree, we get mo' dan one.
SHOGO: Sometimes dis tree, sometimes dat tree, crying.
AKI: You neva say she was crying.
SHOGO: Oh, she always crying. I mean, like, she no go "BOOHOO." She jus' go "hooooooo." Soft, sad kine crying. Da firs' time I wen' see her, I shiishii in my pants. Was so spooky.
AKI: Japanee obake?

SHOGO: Dat I dunno yet, 'cause her hair long, eh, and kinna cova her face. Funny, no. She no let me see da face. And da clothes she wear, I cannot tell if kimono or muumuu.
AKI: Shogo, da wata you drink—diff'rent from da kine odda people drink?
SHOGO: I dunno. I jus' drink da rain wata from da barrel.
AKI: You drink beer or sake, da kine hard liquor?
SHOGO: No, why? Jus' wata and tea. (*The sound of a jalopy offstage. The sound becomes louder as the car approaches. The engine keeps running.*) You faddah dem wen' come home.
AKI: Whose car dat?
SHOGO: Das da Kajiwara boy. Da family wen' scrape up some money to get da jalopy, so sometimes he drive around like one taxi. . . . Aki, you come wit' me one night, so you can see da obake, okay?
AKI: Huh? Oh, yeah, yeah.
SHOGO: You promise? Cross you heart, faddah, muddah die?
AKI: Yeah, I promise.
SHOGO: Cross you heart.
AKI: Cross my heart, faddah, muddah die.
   (AKI *does so, but his eyes look offstage as* TOSH *and* KAZUO *approach and the jalopy rumbles off.* TOSH *helps* KAZUO *toward the house.* MIKAME *comes out.*)
TOSH: Look, Otōsan. Aki came home.
MIKAME: Okaeri.
AKI: Hello, Otōsan.
KAZUO: (*To* TOSH) Take me in the house. Hayō.
MIKAME: Was everything okay?
   (KAZUO, TOSH *and* MIKAME *enter the house.*)
SHOGO: You faddah sure wen' get weak, yeah. He used to be so strong, but now . . . I been working fo' him since you wen' Honolulu. He was one hard worka.
AKI: Yeah, and you see wat wen' happen to him.
   (TOSH *comes out.*)
TOSH: Aeh, Aki.
AKI: Tosh. A few years, yeah. You look good.
TOSH: You too.
AKI: Nah, I no take care myself.
TOSH: T'anks for coming.
AKI: Aeh, you my bruddah, eh.
   (MIKAME *brings out a bowl and chopsticks.*)

MIKAME: Shogo, come here and eat.
SHOGO: Oh, thank you.
(*He sits at the round table on the porch and eats.*)
AKI: I'm not hungry right now, Okāsan.
(MIKAME *reenters the house.* AKI *motions and* TOSH *follows, away from* SHOGO.)
How's da old man?
TOSH: Well, I been taking him to Docta Hayashi. No change. Otōsan not going get betta. Blood circulation real bad in his legs. Da blood not flowing good so because a dat, he get da pain in his legs. I dunno but I guess da pain is real bad, 'cause you know da old man, he tough, but dis time . . .
AKI: No mo' medicine?
TOSH: Nuttin' dat can fix him up. He gotta live wit' it. Going only get worse. But he stubborn, eh. Wheelchair li'dat, he no like. Anyway, wat good one wheelchair on dis kine rough ground.
AKI: I guess his body wen' jus' give out.
TOSH: He no going die, he jus' no can be da way he was befo'. Kinna like one cripple now.
AKI: I wonda . . .
TOSH: Wat?
AKI: I wonda . . . if I neva go Honolulu . . .
(TOMI *enters.*)
TOMI: Hi, Tosh.
TOSH: Tomi. Aeh, look who here.
AKI: Tomi Ishitani?
TOMI: Oh, Aki.
TOSH: Tomi been helping Mama since da old man got really bad.
AKI: T'anks, eh, Tomi.
TOSH: Aki neva change much, yeah.
TOMI: Little bit mo' skinny maybe.
AKI: Aeh, you jus' like my muddah, 's wat she said, too. How's da family?
TOMI: Good. I betta go in and help.
(*She enters the house.*)
AKI: She was always kinna shy, yeah.
TOSH: Mama depend on her plenny. And Tomi get along pretty good wit' Otōsan.
AKI: So wat we going do wit' da old man?
TOSH: Take him to Honolulu.

AKI: He not going.
TOSH: Well, maybe he might listen to you.
AKI: You lōlō or wat? He hate my guts.
TOSH: But you da oldest son, so I figga you get mo' pull dan me. Aki, no mo' future in Kona. You know dat. 'S why you wen' leave.
AKI: 'S not da only reason. Aeh, let's face it. I jus' wanted to have a good time.
TOSH: No, 's not true.
AKI: Okay. I went to Honolulu so I could become one docta. But da university neva like take me wit' my tird-grade education. Tosh, soon as I hit da big city, I wen' start gambling. Funny how one tedesuke like me can find odda tedesukes doing nuttin' but gambling and having a good time.
TOSH: But you doing good now.
AKI: I dunno why I wen' come. Wat I can do or say? You saw da old man— he neva even look at me.
TOSH: You and me, togedda, we can convince dem we all gotta move to Honolulu. 'Cause I gotta go one way or da odda. Even if I gotta leave dem by demself.
AKI: And da old man and old lady gotta suffa.
TOSH: Wat you like I do? You da oldest son, you da one supposed to take care a dem, not me. Nobody stopping you, you can come back and live wit' dem. Den I can go to Honolulu. Wat about dat?
AKI: Yeah, yeah.
TOSH: I . . . ah . . . I dunno. . . No listen to me.
AKI: I no blame you. It's tough.
TOSH: I wen' tell Mama I wanted to go to Honolulu and take dem, too.
AKI: Well, wat she said?
TOSH: She no like go.
AKI: Of course. 'S undastood. Wat a mess. I dunno. I dunno.
(MIKAME *emerges*.)
SHOGO: Oh, Okusan, gottsōsama, gottsōsama.
(*He takes his bowl into the house*.)
MIKAME: Toshio, help Otōsan. He wants to go to the outhouse.
AKI: You want me to help?
MIKAME: No, Toshio and Shogo. They know how.
(TOSH *enters the house*.)
AKI: Every time Otōsan has to go, somebody has to help him?
MIKAME: He can't walk there by himself.

AKI: In Honolulu, the toilets are in the house. Easier for him.
(TOSH *and* SHOGO *help* KAZUO *out and take him off.* TOMI *comes out too.* MIKAME *reenters the house.*)
TOMI: Must be nice, eh, living in da city.
AKI: Oh, yeah, no can beat it. Get electricity. No need kerosene lamp. Aeh, you know how many movie teaters get in da city?
TOMI: How many?
AKI: Too many to count. And not silent kine, eidda. Talking pictures. Da modern age, you know. All kine good stuff in Honolulu. If you eva come to da city, I can show you around.
TOMI: Maybe someday.
AKI: You looking good.
TOMI: Me? Jōdan da nai. I not dressed to go to one party.
AKI: I no mean da clothes. You look real, real . . . strong.
TOMI: Well, I can pack one hundred-pound bag of coffee beans myself.
AKI: Yeah, 's wat I mean. I bet you get good appetite.
TOMI: Why you say dat? I look fat to you?
AKI: No, no, you look, ah, healthy, real healthy. 'S good, living in da country you gotta be healthy. How long my faddah going stay in da outhouse? You know, da bugga get tight ass. I bet he constipated and his unko no like come out.
TOMI: (*Hitting him on the arm.*) You terrible. 'S your faddah.
AKI: So? He no can get stuck shit?
TOMI: You terrible.
AKI: Aeh, no hit me again, eh. Sore, you know.
TOMI: You big faka. I neva hit you hard.
AKI: Aeh, no kid yourself. You get muscles. You tough.
TOMI: Dere, I tink he finish. Tosh wen' in get him.
AKI: My poor bruddah. Stink like-a hell inside. No can breathe in dere. Choke, choke.
TOMI: (*Holding back laughter.*) Stop it.
AKI: See, you know, you like laugh, go, laugh, no hold back, bambai you shiishii in you pants.
TOMI: (*Hits him.*) You bad.
(SHOGO *and* TOSH *help* KAZUO *into the house.*)
AKI: I tink I going walk around da farm.
(*He exits.* SHOGO *emerges.*)
SHOGO: Where he going?
TOMI: Jus' look around.

SHOGO: Aki, you like I go wit' you?
(*He also exits.* TOSH *comes out.*)
TOSH: Where dey going?
TOMI: Aki like see da place.
TOSH: Nuttin' to see.
TOMI: He still like kid around, yeah, da guy.
TOSH: I dunno.
TOMI: Jokey bugga. He get girlfriend in Honolulu?
TOSH: I neva ask.
MIKAME: (*From inside.*) Toshio!
TOSH: Hai.
(*He goes back in.* TOMI *opens the door as* TOSH *brings out* KAZUO *and sits him in the rocking chair.* MIKAME *follows.*)
KAZUO: Where Shogo? Is he working?
TOSH: He's with Aki.
KAZUO: What for?
TOSH: Aki wanted to see the farm again.
KAZUO: Who told him to come back? Better if he stayed in Honolulu. We don't need him here.
MIKAME: Don't be silly. He's your son. It's good he's home.
KAZUO: What does he want? Money?
MIKAME: Why don't you ask him?
KAZUO: I don't have time to talk to him. Time for me to get out in the field. Where's Shogo? Shogo! Shogo!
TOSH: What're you going to do in the field?
KAZUO: Work. Shogo! Shogo!
TOSH: What kind of work?
KAZUO: Baka, don't ask stupid qustions. Take me out there.
TOSH: How? On my back? I can push you out in the wheelbarrow.
KAZUO: Never mind. I can go myself. (*He grabs a post and tries to lift himself but drops back in the chair.*)
MIKAME: Abunai. Be careful. Toshio, help him.
(AKI *and* SHOGO *return.*)
SHOGO: Kamiya-san, you called me?
KAZUO: No! Go back and work. What are you loafing for? Hayō, hayō, work, work.
SHOGO: Hai. (*He races off.*)
AKI: Otōsan, the farm looks good.
(KAZUO *looks away.*)

MIKAME: Akira, come inside and eat.
AKI: That's okay. I'm not hungry.
MIKAME: Come in.
   (AKI *enters with* MIKAME, *followed by* TOSH.)
TOMI: Kamiya-san, want me to massage your legs?
   (*He grunts and nods.* AKI *watches from the screen door.*)
TOMI: Feel better?
   (KAZUO *grunts and nods again. Lights fade to black.*)

Scene 3

(*The next day, midmorning.* AKI *is sawing wood, trying to build a primitive walker.* HARUKO *enters.*)

HARUKO: Hi, Aki.
AKI: Hi.
HARUKO: Well, you know who me?
AKI: Ah, you look familiar but . . .
HARUKO: You. . . . Haruko . . . Tomi's sista.
AKI: Oh, Haruko, oh. Boy, you sure wen' grow up. Not potot anymo'. Yeah, big girl now.
HARUKO: Tomi was saying las' night you wen' come home. But you going back to Honolulu, yeah?
AKI: Oh yeah. No can stay in one dead place like Kona.
HARUKO: I know. I hate living here. All da boys tedesuke. No mo' nuttin' fo' do. No mo' fun.
AKI: I know how you feel.
HARUKO: Wat you doing?
AKI: I making someting fo' my faddah. Who you wen' come see?
HARUKO: You.
AKI: Me? Why?
HARUKO: Well, I neva see you long time.
AKI: I know, you was jus' one kid wen I wen' Honolulu.
HARUKO: Well, dat was long time ago.
AKI: Wat you doing now? You working?
HARUKO: Yeah, I go to da Franklin house to do da laundry.
AKI: Laundry? 'S one job fo' one old lady.
HARUKO: I know. So stupid.
AKI: You too young and pretty fo' dat.

HARUKO: You tink I pretty?
AKI: Oh yeah.
HARUKO: Pretty as da Honolulu girls?
AKI: You betta looking. Da Honolulu girls put on too much makeup, deir hair all funny kine and dey wear da stink kine perfume.
(HARUKO *comes close and puts her arms around* AKI.)
HARUKO: How I smell?
AKI: Hmmm, like pīkake afta one light morning rain.
HARUKO: Hontō?
AKI: Yeah, 's da truth. You hundred times betta dan da Honolulu girls. You know, if you was living in Honolulu, you could be a clerk in one big fancy store or a waitress in one nice restaurant where you can get big tips.
HARUKO: Honolulu is nice, yeah.
AKI: I love da city. You know, get gas stoves. Da firs' time I wen' see one gas stove, I neva know wat fo' do. You shoulda seen me scratching my head, trying to figga out how da ting work. Kinna shame, yeah, real country jack. But I wen' learn fas'. Gas stove, electric lights, da toilet in da house, not outside like here. Wat mo' you like?
HARUKO: Yes, yes, yes, yes.
(*She spins around in a circle, her skirt flaring out.* TOMI *enters.*)
AKI: Hi, Tomi.
TOMI: Haru, wat you doing here? You suppose to be at da Franklin house.
HARUKO: I no can say hello to Aki? How long I no see him.
TOMI: You faddah inside?
AKI: No. He stay out in da field wit' Shogo and Tosh and my muddah. Dey digging up some weeds, I tink.
TOMI: Oh, den I can clean up some tings in da house. Haru, hurry up and go.
HARUKO: I get time.
(TOMI *enters the house.*)
HARUKO: Aki, tonight we go meet someplace. I like talk some mo' about Honolulu.
AKI: Well, I guess so. You like I come to you house?
HARUKO: No. I come here. Afta dinna. If you can wait out here on da porch.
AKI: Okay.
HARUKO: Going be one full moon tonight.
(*She runs off.* AKI *returns to his work.* TOMI *emerges with a blanket, which she airs out on a clothes wire.*)

AKI: How old you sista now?

TOMI: She wen' jus' make eighteen dis year, but she still one baby.

AKI: How old you?

TOMI: Me? You know.

AKI: I dunno.

TOMI: Den I no going tell you.

AKI: Wassa matta, hazukashii? No need be shame.

TOMI: Mind your own business.

AKI: Sassy, eh, you.

TOMI: You sassy.

AKI: T'anks fo' helping da family.

TOMI: Well, not free, you know. Dey pay me some.

AKI: Yeah, but not enough to be around my faddah.

TOMI: He's okay. Little bit hard head but.

AKI: If I tell you someting, you can keep one secret?

TOMI: Yeah, wat?

AKI: Tosh and me going take my muddah and faddah to Honolulu.

TOMI: Hontō? You bull liar.

AKI: No, fo' real.

TOMI: Why?

AKI: Gotta. Tosh like move to Honolulu, too, so we no can leave da old folks here by demself.

TOMI: Your faddah said okay? He neva say nuttin'.

AKI: 'S because he dunno yet.

TOMI: Why you telling me fo'?

AKI: Well, wat you tink? Good idea, eh.

TOMI: I dunno. Your faddah not going.

AKI: You see how helpless he stay. He gotta go wit' Tosh and me. And wat people going say if we jus' leave him and my muddah here all by demself. Shame, eh. We gotta take care a da folks, but dey gotta come wit' us.

TOMI: Why you no come back Kona? Not dat bad.

AKI: You say dat because you neva been to Honolulu. You dunno. If you wen' to Honolulu, you would change you mind. At leas' you get big family, you lucky, no need worry like me.

TOMI: Yeah, but gotta feed four boys and two girls, so . . .

AKI: You rememba my old bruddah, Kishiyo?

TOMI: No.

AKI: He was couple years olda dan me. I was about five wen he wen' die. Sick. But da ting was, my faddah really loved Kishiyo, da oldest son and all dat, you know. So I not really da numba one son, see. Sometimes I tink why da hell Kashiyo had to die. Jam everyting up. Me, hard luck.

TOMI: Wat, you one big baby? No feel sorry for yourself. You and Tosh strong and healthy, and at leas' your folks still alive. Look at Shogo. His faddah wen' desert him and his muddah and run away to da mainland. And now Shogo's muddah ma-ke, so only himself. I feel sorry for him.

AKI: Yeah, he get one hard-luck story, but he too stupid to know he get hard luck, so no count. Me, I know I get hard luck.

TOMI: I no can listen to one sissy. (*She reenters the house.*)

AKI: Sissy? Wat sissy get to do wit' dis? Sissy? Jus' because I get one hard-luck story?

(SHOGO *enters.*)

SHOGO: You get hard luck, Aki?

AKI: Wat? Aeh, you pau work already?

SHOGO: No, you faddah like I bring some wata.

AKI: Why he no come get 'um himself.

SHOGO: You know why, kawaisō, eh.

AKI: Kawaisō? You feel sorry fo' my faddah? Wit' his stone face and mean mout' and kichigai ideas?

SHOGO: Oh, but Aki, I rememba wen he was so strong and always work like-a hell. My muddah always used to tell me how you faddah wen' help her plenny wen my old man wen' run away. My faddah used to always lose money gambling. People look down on us, but you faddah always try help my muddah and me. My muddah neva fo'get.

(TOMI *opens the door and hands a water jug to* SHOGO.)

SHOGO: Oh, arigatō. (*To* AKI.) You lucky you get one good faddah.

(SHOGO *trots off.*)

TOMI: Shogo not one sissy.

(*She closes the door behind her. Lights fade to black.*)

Scene 4

(*Early evening. Dinner is over.* MIKAME *opens the door so* TOSH *can help* KAZUO *outside to sit.* MIKAME *puts a kerosene lamp on the table.*)

KAZUO: Toshio, make sure we have enough Pilipino workers to help pick the coffee. Almost time.

TOSH: We have plenty of time yet. Don't worry.

KAZUO: Baka. We have to worry. The South Kona coffee farmers pick way before us. They may take all the workers away.

TOSH: No. We have our regulars.

KAZUO: What if they don't want to pick for us? What if they go to Honolulu?

(AKI *listens at the screen door.*)

TOSH: What're you worried about? Year after year we always manage.

KAZUO: Because I worry, that's why. I'm not nonki like you. If I had to depend on you to handle everything, nothing would get done.

MIKAME: That's not true. Without Toshio you couldn't do anything. He handles all the details, does all the heavy work, manages the Pilipino boys. . . .

TOSH: Never mind, Okāsan, it doesn't matter anymore.

(AKI *comes out.*)

AKI: Otōsan, I made something for you today.

MIKAME: What?

AKI: I thought it was something Otōsan could use.

MIKAME: Where is it?

AKI: Otōsan, you want to see it?

MIKAME: Of course he does. Bring it here.

(AKI *leaps off the porch to the side of the house.* KAZUO *glares at* MIKAME.) Why are you looking at me like that? I'm your wife, not your dog.

(AKI *returns with the wooden walker. He demonstrates.*)

AKI: See, Otōsan. You can use it to walk around, like this. It's very strong. You can put all your weight on it. Toshio and Shogo don't have to help you. (*He puts the walker in front of* KAZUO.)

MIKAME: Oh, nice.

KAZUO: Dame kore. Iran!

(KAZUO *pushes the walker off the porch disgustedly.* AKI *walks off to the side of the stage.* TOSH *picks up the walker and takes it to the side of the house, then joins* AKI.)

AKI: I wen' work all day on dat damn ting.

TOSH: He probably not strong enough to use right now anyway.

AKI: He like ack tough, I can ack tough, too.

TOSH: Why we no tell 'um now. Tell 'um you and me going to Honolulu and he and Okāsan gotta go wit' us. Da Okazaki family like buy our lease. I get everyting all set to go.

AKI: Wat about Okāsan?

TOSH: Well, she know if we go, den dey gotta come wit' us. Shōganai, eh. She not hard head like da old man.
AKI: I dunno. She like Kona too.
TOSH: But she mo' realistic. And you know her, she can adjust easy. 'S one ting good about her. We go tell da old man tonight.
AKI: No. Mo' betta daytime. Wit' da blue sky and da bright sun. I no like da night or shadow covering his face. And if get tears, da sun going dry 'um up quick.
TOSH: Okay. But I no can hold back. I ready to bust.
AKI: No worry. He going get 'um right between da eyes.
(*Lights down.*)

Scene 5

(*Later that evening. A moonlit area at stage left downstage. Offstage the sound of* HARUKO's *laughter. She enters with a blanket, followed by* AKI.)

HARUKO: Ova here good. (*She spreads the blanket and sits.*) See, I told you. Full moon. (*She reaches out and grabs* AKI *by the arm and pulls him down.*) Oh, you so tight. How come?
AKI: Aaahhh, my old man wen' give me one headache.
HARUKO: Oh, you poor ting. (*She gently massages his temples.*) Good?
AKI: Oh, yeah. Hmmmm.
(HARUKO *purposely brushes her long hair against his face, then massages his shoulders.*)
HARUKO: You gotta relax your shoulders. (*She hums the song "I'll See You in My Dreams," then sways sensuously with the song.*) Tell me mo' about Honolulu.
AKI: Well, lotta cars on da streets. Get some nice beaches.
HARUKO: Da haole girls beautiful, yeah?
AKI: Nah. Dey jus' tall.
HARUKO: You go to dances?
AKI: Dances? Wat, bon dance?
HARUKO: You know, in nightclubs, like in da moving pictures.
AKI: Me? No, too busy.
HARUKO: Doing wat?
AKI: Working. Night and day I working. Isogashii. No mo' res'.

HARUKO: If I was in Honolulu, I no let you work so hard. You gotta play, too. I would take you dancing. You know how, eh?
AKI: Dancing? No, my legs too bowlegged.
HARUKO: Come, I show you. Easy.
AKI: No, no, too clumsy.
HARUKO: Jus' hold me like dis. (*She wraps his arms around her.*) See. Now all you gotta do is move nice and easy. Ouch!
AKI: Sorry.
HARUKO: Relax, no need move your feet. See, see. (*She clings to him and sways gently.*) I love American songs betta dan Japanee songs. I hear all da songs at da Franklin house. Da Franklin okusan always singing and playing da piano. (*She sings softly a few bars of "I'll See You in My Dreams."*)
AKI: You smell nice.

(HARUKO *puts her lips up to* AKI. *He pulls his head back to look at her pursed lips. She gently holds the back of his head and brings their lips together in a lingering kiss.*)

HARUKO: Aki, oh, Aki. . . . Da haole girls betta dan me?
AKI: No, you da bes'.
HARUKO: Wat you like bes' about me?
AKI: Everyting.
HARUKO: My legs, you like my legs?
AKI: Well . . . (She slowly lifts her skirt up to her thighs.)
HARUKO: See, I no mo' daikon legs, eh?
AKI: No.
HARUKO: You like see da res' of me?
AKI: Well . . . I . . . ah . . .

(HARUKO *drops her dress and stands in her full slip. She kisses him again and they go down on the blanket.*)

HARUKO: Life in Kona is hard, yeah. 'S why you wen' leave. I wen' cry dat time, you know.
AKI: Yeah? Why?
HARUKO: Because I loved you. I always loved you.
AKI: But you was only twelve dat time.
HARUKO: So? I can still love. You know Juliet was only fourteen wen she wen' fall in love wit' Romeo.
AKI: Yeah? So wat wen' happen to dis Juliet?
HARUKO: Oh, her parents and Romeo's parents no like dey get married, so dey hadda die in each odda's arms.

AKI: Wat, hara-kiri?
HARUKO: Someting li'dat.
AKI: So you like I commit suicide?
HARUKO: No, silly. I jus' telling you dat Juliet was only fourteen, and I already eighteen. Me not one baby, I get all da feeling of one woman. And my body hungry for you.
(*She rubs her body sensuously against* AKI.)
AKI: Aeh, I jus' wen' eat dinna, so no feel bad if my body not hungry right now.
HARUKO: Aki, wen you go back to Honolulu . . . I no like da odda Kona boys. Dey all so dumb and backward. Jus' like babies. You live in da city now, you know all about life.
(*They kiss again. Now* HARUKO *rises and lets her slip fall to to the ground. She stands seductively in her old-fashioned brassiere and panties.*)
Aki, come take off my tings for me. I waiting.
SHOGO: (*Far offstage right.*) Aki! Aki!
HARUKO: Aeeiihh, who dat? (*She gathers her clothes and ducks off upstage left.*)
AKI: Haruko, wait.
(*He grabs the blanket as* SHOGO *scurries in from upstage right.* SHOGO, *with a lantern, stops halfway and looks offstage, then continues to proceed in the direction of* HARUKO's *exit. He turns to see* AKI.)
SHOGO: Aki, 's you?
AKI: Shogo, wat you doing here?
SHOGO: Aki, you wen' promise you going see da obake wit' me.
AKI: Yeah, but I neva say now.
SHOGO: But Aki, you dunno. Jus' now, little while ago, I wen' see da obake again.
AKI: And wat? She wen' talk to you?
SHOGO: No, but she was diff'rent tonight. She was standing in da moonlight again, but dis time funny kine. She was wearing only one brassiere and panties.
AKI: Shogo, you sure was one ghost?
SHOGO: Oh yeah, But I wonda wat da meaning, you know, why she only had on undawear.
AKI: Aeh, das da real mystery, eh. We go back.
SHOGO: No, no, I like you see da obake, too.
AKI: I tink da obake wen' home already. And I bet she get her clothes on, too, by now.

SHOGO: Wait. Look, look. (*He points over the audience. They stare intently.*)
AKI: Wat? I no see nuttin'.
SHOGO: You hear dat?
AKI: I no hear nuttin'.
SHOGO: 'S wat I mean. Nuttin'. Too quiet. 'S wen da obake come out, and da birds and animals run away. Wat dat ova dere? See, da red eyes, da red eyes.
AKI: I no see no red eyes. Probably one mongoose.
SHOGO: You hear dat, you hear?
AKI: Wat? I no hear nuttin'. You jus' said, too quiet.
SHOGO: You no hear somebody crying, one lady. So clear, you no hear?
AKI: Nobody crying.
SHOGO: Someting wrong wit' you ears.
AKI: Aeh, my ears good; my muddah wen' clean 'um today.
(SHOGO's *eyes widen; his face contorts.* AKI *tries to see what* SHOGO *sees.*)
SHOGO: Oooooohhhhhh, oooohhhhh.
AKI: Wat, wat?
SHOGO: Look out, look out!
(SHOGO *runs off, wailing.* AKI *looks around, confused, spooked, then suddenly exits. Lights fade to black.*)

Scene 6

(*The next day. Afternoon.* MIKAME *and* KAZUO *are seated on the porch.*)

MIKAME: Nice to see Akira and Toshio working together out there. Brings back memories. They're strong boys. Akira is stronger.... He has the body of a farmer but... Toshio is very sensitive, a good boy. Oyakoko. Devoted to us but—
KAZUO: I cannot die yet.
MIKAME: What?
KAZUO: I still have things to do.
MIKAME: You're not going to die.
KAZUO: I still have to go back to Kumamoto and put senkō on my parents' grave.
MIKAME: Yes, yes, someday.
KAZUO: Did the doctor say I was going to die?

MIKAME: No, of course not.
KAZUO: Why are my legs so bad?
MIKAME: He told you why.
KAZUO: What did he tell you?
MIKAME: The same thing. I was there with you.
KAZUO: Why can't the doctor fix it?
MIKAME: Doctors don't know how yet.
KAZUO: Work is the only thing I'm good for.
MIKAME: You worked hard all your life. Let others work for you now.
KAZUO: Why did Akira return? Did he say? What does he want?
MIKAME: I asked, but he didn't say.
KAZUO: What do you mean? He must have said something. . . . If he wants to come back . . . he can. He can come home.
MIKAME: Tell him that. It might help.
KAZUO: No. I don't have to say a word. He knows me. Maybe that's why he's working in the field with Toshio. To show me he wants to come home. To admit he was wrong to leave in the first place. I wish I could go out there right now and work with them, side by side. (*He hits his calves repeatedly in frustration.*) I have to work. I must work.
MIKAME: You will, once you get better.
KAZUO: When I left Japan, I told my mother not to worry. I said I would come home once I made enough money to take care of her. But she couldn't wait for me. I have to go back to burn incense at her grave and ask her to forgive me.
MIKAME: She understands.

(KAZUO *massages his calves.*)

KAZUO: I'll make my legs get better. Somehow I will be strong again. The coffee crop will be good this year. I think one tree can fill one bag of coffee beans. If I can pick coffee the way I used to, then we can hire one less worker and save a little that way. In the off season I want to go back and work in the sugarcane fields for the haole company. Toshio is good in the cane fields; the haole bosses like him.
MIKAME: Tell him you're proud of him. That would make him happy. Sometimes we have to say things like that.
KAZUO: That's not the kind of people we are. They know that.

(AKI *and* TOSH *enter in work clothes with hoes. They stop at a distance.*)

AKI: I tell you dat Shogo little off.
TOSH: Wat? And his obake wen' scare you?
AKI: Nah. Obake? Big joke.

TOSH: Aeh, look da old man massaging his legs. He used to be so strong. Now look.

AKI: Aeh, no feel sorry fo' him. You pity him and pau, you no can buck him. Rememba, he da one holding you back, he da one keeping you in Kona.

TOSH: I know, I know.

AKI: So da Okazaki family ready to buy da lease from us?

TOSH: Yeah. But Otōsan gotta give up and let go. Or else no good.

AKI: How 'bout tomorrow you and me, we tell da old man wat we like do? Shoot da works.

TOSH: Might as well. No use wait.

KAZUO: Why are those two standing there like idiots? They should be working.

MIKAME: No, I want Toshio to take me to the store.

KAZUO: Not now. What for?

MIKAME: Chicken heka tonight—for Akira.

KAZUO: Niga-haru. Feed him daikon and rice; that's all he's worth.

MIKAME: He's your son. We have to welcome him home.

KAZUO: Who's going to watch over me?

MIKAME: Akira will be here.

KAZUO: No, no. Where's Tomi? Why didn't you tell her to come?

MIKAME: She can't be here every day for you. Toshio!

TOSH: What?

MIKAME: Go with me to Komo Store. Ima.

TOSH: Hai.

MIKAME: Akira, go catch a chicken in the field. We're going to have chicken heka tonight.

AKI: Oh? Who's coming?

MIKAME: For you.

AKI: Me?

TOSH: Wow, big shot, eh, you.

MIKAME: If Otōsan needs you, he'll call out.

AKI: Hai. Okay. I'm going to catch the fattest chicken I can find.

TOSH: You sure you can? You been in da city too long, maybe. I no tink you can catch up wit' da chickens.

AKI: Aeh, baby bruddah, no worry about me. Here I go.
(*He trots off.*)

MIKAME: Let's go and come back quick. (*To* KAZUO.) Call Akira if you need to go to the outhouse. We'll be right back.

(MIKAME *and* TOSH *exit.* KAZUO *massages his legs. He maneuvers the round table toward him, then slowly rises with his weight on the table. His feeble and pained legs can hardly hold him up. He drops back in the chair. But he is determined. Once more he rises against the table. He tries to step out, but the pain causes him to crumble and tumble off the porch. He lies motionless on the ground. After a while,* AKI *returns. He stops at the side of the house and doesn't see his father on the porch.*)

AKI: Otōsan . . . Otōsan. (*He comes to the front of the house and sees* KAZUO.) Otōsan! (*He hurries to* KAZUO.) Otōsan, Otōsan, wat you did! Wat da hell you was doing!

(AKI *tries to help, but* KAZUO *suddenly jerks his elbow back, hitting* AKI, *causing him to fall backward.*)

You stupid! You so stupid!

(KAZUO *lies helpless on the ground as lights fade to black.*)

ACT TWO
Scene 1

(*The next morning.* TOSH *and* AKI *emerge from the house.*)

TOSH: Good ting da old man was not hurt bad.

AKI: Yeah, I like slap his head fo' making me sweat li'dat. Wen I wen' find him, I tought he was dead.

TOSH: Wat da hell he was tinking, trying to walk around.

AKI: He probably wanted to get hurt, so everybody feel sorry fo' him. Well, not me. If he wen' die or gotta go hospital, den I was going be da bad guy. 'S wat he wanted. People would ask me, "Aki, how come you neva take care you faddah?" And I going look like one damn fool if I tell dem, "Aeh, not my fault, I was out chasing one chicken."

TOSH: You tink wen we all move to Honolulu, people going call us damn fools?

AKI: Yeah, some a dem, da old futheads. But you gotta rememba—dis is like one war between Japan and America.

TOSH: Wat?

AKI: See, Okāsan and Otōsan and all da odda people who wen' come from Japan, dey get deir own ideas about how to live, ideas from Japan. I no blame dem. 'S how dey was raised. Dey dunno any betta. But us guys, eh, we born in Hawai'i. We American citizens, right? We no can live

da old-fashion Japan way. We gotta tink like Americans. Japan is da past.
TOSH: Yeah, but da Japan way is strong, eh, hard to buck da old man.
AKI: Nemmine dat. No fo'get, we gotta win da war, we gotta win da war.
TOSH: (*He salutes.*) Yessir, General Kamiya.
AKI: Now where Sergeant Shogo?
TOSH: Probably still at da Cameron ranch.
  (*He prepares the spraying equipment.*)
AKI: You tink Shogo like go to Honolulu wit' us?
TOSH: I dunno, why?
AKI: I feel sorry fo' him. He no mo' nobody, eh. He can come wit' us.
TOSH: You can ask, no harm.
  (TOMI *enters.*)
AKI: Aeh, Tomi.
TOSH: Hi, Tomi.
TOMI: Hi, your faddah feeling betta?
TOSH: Oh yeah, cranky as eva.
TOMI: If he can complain, den I guess he's okay. Lucky, no, he neva get hurt bad.
AKI: Yeah, he only wanted to give me one heart attack.
TOSH: Well, I going out firs'.
  (*He puts the spraying equipment on his back, then ties a bandana over his nose and mouth and exits.*)
AKI: Watch out how you spray da poison on da tall grass.
TOMI: I betta go see your faddah.
AKI: I dunno how you take it.
TOMI: Wat?
AKI: My faddah no get you crazy?
TOMI: No. He get hard head, and he like ack bossy, and he fut around da house and no say "excuse," but odda dan dat, he jus' like one angel.
AKI: You funny, you know dat, you funny. You make me laugh. I neva tought you was funny. You get boyfriend?
TOMI: You get da nerve to ask.
AKI: Aeh, I get balls, you know. 'S two tings I get.
TOMI: You bad, you real bad.
AKI: Wen you going get married?
TOMI: Mind your own business. . . . Wat about you?
AKI: Wat?

TOMI: Get married.
AKI: I gotta find da right girl firs'.
TOMI: Get plenny girls on Oʻahu.
AKI: Yeah, and at leas' ten like I marry dem. But dey not my type.
TOMI: Wat your type?
   (MIKAME *comes out in work clothes.*)
   Oh, Okusan, how is . . .
MIKAME: He's fine. Resting well.
TOMI: I better go in.
MIKAME: Yes, thank you, he'll be happy to see you.
   (TOMI *enters the house.*)
AKI: Otōsan gets along well with Tomi.
MIKAME: She's patient with him. Her family raised her well. She knows how to treat her elders.
   (*She wears a wide-brim hat and bandana on her face.* AKI *puts a bandana on his face, too, and they grab their hoes and exit.*)

Scene 2

(*That evening. Downstage at left there is a spot of light.* HARUKO *enters the light, preening as if in front of a mirror.* TOMI *enters the light.*)

TOMI: Wat you doing?
HARUKO: Wat you tink? I going out. I get one date.
TOMI: Wit' who?
HARUKO: Somebody.
TOMI: Who?
HARUKO: My boyfriend.
TOMI: Yukito?
HARUKO: Yukito? No, he so stupid. I no like da kine tedesuke. My boyfriend is Aki Kamiya.
TOMI: Aki?
HARUKO: Yes, he going take me to Honolulu.
TOMI: Wat?
HARUKO: Yes, and we going get married dere.
TOMI: He said he going marry you?
HARUKO: Not yet, but he going.

TOMI: And he said he taking you?
HARUKO: Yeah.
TOMI: I no believe you.
HARUKO: You neva believe me—about anyting.
TOMI: Why should Aki tell you all dose tings?
HARUKO: Because he love me.
TOMI: Aki not da type to say da kine.
HARUKO: You jealous.
TOMI: Aki no love you.
HARUKO: We wen' make love.
TOMI: No lie.
HARUKO: We did. On his farm. Out where nobody wen' see us. We wen' kiss and we wen'—
TOMI: Shut up.
HARUKO: Well, you wen' ask. Why you ask for?
TOMI: No go out tonight.
HARUKO: I can go if I like. You no can stop me.
TOMI: Aki no good for you.
HARUKO: Wat you know. Why, you like him for yourself?
TOMI: No be silly.
HARUKO: Den no bodda me. Aki waiting, I gotta go.
(HARUKO *exits. Lights fade to black.*)

Scene 3

(*Later that evening. Downstage left again. This time there is a moonlit spot.* AKI *and* HARUKO *enter with a blanket.*)

AKI: Howzit ova here. Nice, eh.
HARUKO: I like stay any place wit' you.
(*They sit.* HARUKO *snuggles up to him.*) I hope nobody bodda us dis time.
AKI: No worry. I wen' give Shogo money to go see one moving picture at Hōlualoa. He wen' jump on his donkey and go.
HARUKO: How come you neva take me instead?
AKI: Oh, I tought you radda come here.
HARUKO: Yeah. Dis mo' romantic. Da moon in Honolulu mo' nice dan dis?
AKI: I dunno, I neva notice da moon ova Honolulu.

HARUKO: I can hardly wait till you take me to Honolulu.
AKI: Yeah, and . . . wat you jus' said?
HARUKO: Where you go, I go.
AKI: To Honolulu?
(*She nods.*)
No can. My folks going live wit' me.
HARUKO: Your folks? Why you like old people stay wit' you? If we live togedda, we can have so much fun. We can make love every night. We no like live wit' old people. Not us.
AKI: Wat you folks going say?
HARUKO: Dey no need know . . till we get married.
AKI: Married?
HARUKO: We love each odda, so we gotta get married.
AKI: Wait, wait, wait. . . . You going too fas' fo' me.
HARUKO: Nemmine, jus' make love to me. (*She kisses him passionately, then slowly slides to the ground.*) Hurry up. . . . Wat you doing? . . . Hurry up. I neva know you was so shy. You like I take off my own clothes? Okay den.
TOMI: (*Far offstage.*) Haruko! Haruko!
AKI: Aeh, who dat?
HARUKO: Sound like Tomi.
AKI: Wat she doing out here?
HARUKO: You know her; she checking up on me.
AKI: How she know you here?
HARUKO: I told her I was coming here for you.
TOMI: (*Closer offstage.*) Haruko!
AKI: We betta get outta here.
HARUKO: Wat for? Let her find us making love.
AKI: No, no, we go, we go.
HARUKO: No. (*She is unbuttoning her dress.*)
AKI: Wat you doing?
HARUKO: I no shame. Let her see me naked and I can tell her we was making love.
AKI: You crazy? Please, please, we go befo' too late. C'mon, c'mon. (*He pulls her up and grabs the blanket.*) Okay, okay, dis way, no talk, sshhh . . . and no tell Tomi we was out here, okay, okay?
(*They exit.* TOMI *enters with a lantern. She looks, picks up a key chain. She exits. Lights fade to black.*)

Scene 4

(The next morning. TOSH *emerges from the side of the house, laughing.* MIKAME *comes out of the house.)*

TOSH: Okāsan, Aki has another surprise.
MIKAME: What?
TOSH: Wait, chotto.
MIKAME: Looks like it might rain today.
TOSH: Maybe a little. Summer shower.
   (AKI *appears from the side of the house, carrying a homemade wooden toilet chair.*)
AKI: Okāsan, look. (*He proudly displays his handiwork.*)
MIKAME: What is it?
AKI: A portable toilet for Otōsan. See. (*He sits on it to demonstrate.*) Instead of carrying him to the outhouse to unko, he can do it with this. Then Tosh can carry the unko to the outhouse.
TOSH: Aeh, how come my job?
AKI: Aeh, me da inventa, so you gotta do da stink job.
MIKAME: I don't know if Otōsan will use it.
AKI: Sure he will. Don't tell him I made it. Tell him Doctor Hayashi had it brought over. It's strong, see.
MIKAME: Hmmm. Save time and trouble.
AKI: Yes, no question about that. Tosh can take it in the house to show Otōsan.
TOSH: Okay, okay.
   (TOSH *packs it inside as* MIKAME *follows him.* AKI *is proud as he struts in front of the house.* JIRO SAKAI *enters.*)
JIRO: Aki, is that you?
   (AKI *turns to see* JIRO, *looking very collegiate. He wears a mustache, and his hair is severely slicked back with pomade.*)
AKI: Aeh, Jiro Sakai?
JIRO: Yes.
AKI: You look diff'rent, but, aeh, I still recognize you, Jiro.
JIRO: I heard you were back. Thought I'd come by to say hello.
AKI: Wat you doing now?
JIRO: I'm just back from the mainland. Going to college. I'll be graduating next year.

AKI: Good fo' you.
JIRO: You still living in Honolulu?
AKI: Yeah.
JIRO: Planning to return to Kona?
AKI: No, Honolulu betta.
JIRO: I know. I feel the same way about the mainland. It's sad but Kona is too backward for me now.
AKI: Yeah? How come?
JIRO: Well, you know. It's hard to relate to Kona people now. I don't have the same interests anymore. Here there's nothing to converse about but mundane things, like the weather, the crops, the family, the neighbors. Right? You've been in Honolulu all this time, you know what I mean. You talk about more important things.
AKI: Yeah, in Honolulu I always talk about sinking da eight ball in da corna pocket.
JIRO: (*Laughs.*) Aki, you're always kidding. That's what I liked about you.
TOSH: (*From inside.*) Aeh, Aki, da old man . . .

(*He comes out and sees* JIRO.)

JIRO: Hi there, Tosh.
TOSH: Yeah, hi.
AKI: Wat about da old man?
TOSH: Nuttin'. I betta hit da field. (*He takes a hoe and departs.*)
JIRO: I still remember those days when you took Tosh and me fishing on the coast.
AKI: Yeah, small kid time. Dat was good fun.
JIRO: Tosh and I were friends then, but now, I don't know. . . . That's what I mean. Like I'm a stranger to my old friends and even my family.
AKI: I know. 'S tough. But people change. Except my old man, he neva change. Still old-style Japan. Jiro, you study on da mainland, mingle wit' da haoles, you going pick up new ideas. You going change, too. No can help.
JIRO: I don't want it to be that way, but . . . some people think I'm a snob, high nose and all that. Yet I don't think I am. It's just that I'm different now. What can I do?

(TOMI *enters.*)

AKI: Hi, Tomi.
JIRO: Tomiko, nice to see you.
TOMI: Hello. (*She enters the house.*)

JIRO: Tomiko, too. When we were kids, she used to talk to me. But since I've been on the mainland, she treats me like an outcast. Other people do the same thing. Have they been avoiding you since you've been back?

AKI: Yeah, but 's because my body smell stink. Nah, nah, nah, I jus' kidding. No can help, eh, 's my style.

JIRO: I know. That's why I can talk to you. What do you think I should do? I can't ask my own brothers. They're just as bad as the other Kona people.

AKI: Well, I tell you, 's da price you pay. You get education, you make new friends. And lotta times you going lose da old friends you had, but 's life, yeah. Jus' no tink your unko no stink because you can talk good English and you parents can only talk Japanese. And be happy you get good bruddahs who wen' keep up da farm so you can go school. You lucky you neva get one lousy bruddah like me. Den you hadda stay home on da farm like Tosh, and no mainland school fo' you. Always t'ank you parents and you bruddahs and you no go wrong.

JIRO: Yes, I can appreciate that.

AKI: So I guess you gotta live on da mainland wit' you new friends.

JIRO: But when I'm on the mainland, I feel uncomfortable because I'm a Japanese in a white man's world.

AKI: Aeh, wait, I tought you was happy on da mainland?

JIRO: Well, some haoles are nice, but a lot of them give me the cold shoulder or act like I'm a worm under their shoe.

AKI: Jiro, you get hit two ways, eh. Lef' uppacut in Kona and right cross on da mainland.

JIRO: That's about it.

AKI: I dunno wat fo' tell you den. Except cova yourself at all times. Keep da arms up at you face and no get caught on da ropes.

JIRO: Maybe it would've been better if I had stayed home like Tosh and not gone to school.

AKI: No, Jiro, 's da wrong way to tink. You gotta walk da tight rope, yeah, but you wen' come dis far, so no give up. Someday, you going be one docta or lawya, I dunno wat. Da Japanese get one good word: Gambare. Right? Gambare. You give 'um all you get all da time. No give up fo' nuttin'.

JIRO: Yes, comes right back to being Japanese, I guess.

AKI: Yup, 's our pride and our problem.

JIRO: I hope I see you before you go back to Honolulu.

AKI: Sure. Any time.
JIRO: Thanks for listening to me, Aki. I think if you had gone to school, you would've been a great philosopher.

(JIRO *exits.* TOSH *returns.*)

AKI: Aeh, wat is one philosopher?
TOSH: I dunno. Da bugga sure love hear himself talk.
AKI: Jiro is okay. Not easy fo' him wen you gotta ack half Japanese and half haole.
TOSH: You neva have to see him every summa wen he come home from school.
AKI: 'S why you like go Honolulu? Because of Jiro?
TOSH: No. But you see how much Jiro wen' learn on da mainland and how stupid me picking coffee in Kona. Da longa I stay here, da worse going be. 'S why I gotta go Honolulu.
AKI: Yeah, yeah, but rememba, I wen' Honolulu, and I mo' stupid now dan befo'. So jus' because you go Honolulu, no mean you going get smart.
TOSH: Aki, you changing your mind? You no going help me tell Otōsan?
AKI: We going tell Otōsan; I gotta tell 'um. 'S my job.
TOSH: Since you da oldest son, I tought you get mo' pull.
AKI: Aeh, aeh, no fo'get dis. I not really da oldest. Kishiyo was da oldest. Too bad he wen' ma-ke. Kishiyo should be da one wit' da responsibility. Kishiyo, why you wen' die fo'. . . . Da folks still put senkō in da shrine fo' him, yeah.
TOSH: Every day. Mama put some rice dere too.
AKI: You know, Shogo get his obake, but we get ours too. Kishiyo.
TOSH: Kishiyo's ghost wen' come see you?
AKI: No, no. Kishiyo wen' ma-ke twenty years ago, but his spirit still stay wit' us. Every day, no miss, senkō and rice fo' Kishiyo. We neva can fo'get him. Kishiyo, you hear me, you take care da folks, so me and Tosh can go Honolulu. But you no can, 'cause you only one spirit.
TOSH: So up to you and me.
AKI: I hate it. You gotta sacrifice you personal freedom fo' da good of da family. 'S right, you gotta do dat. Family duty come firs'. And Otōsan believe in dat. 'S why he love da Chūsingura story so much. Wen da forty-seven loyal samurai wen' give up deir life to avenge deir Lord Asano fo' da honor of da clan—'s da whole Japanese style go back hundreds and hundreds of years. And two pikanini guys like us bucking dat code.
TOSH: But, Aki, Otōsan is not samurai. Jus' one poor dumb farma.

AKI: So? Farmas can be proud, too. You no unnastand dat? Look at Otō-san, he get jus' as much pride as one samurai. 'S why hard. We stealing Otōsan's pride, leaving him wit' nuttin'.

TOSH: So wat you saying? Stay in Kona? Live my whole life here? You asking me to stay so you can go back to Honolulu? I go crazy if I gotta—

AKI: I know, I know. I not asking you to stay. If I go back to Honolulu, you going wit' me. I promise. I guess it's eidda Otōsan or us. And Otōsan gotta lose.

TOSH: We can tell 'um now.

AKI: No, maybe tomorrow or da next day. Humbug he wen' fall down. No good tell him now. We gotta wait little while longa. Give 'um little bit—

(TOMI *comes out.*)

TOMI: Oh, excuse. . . . Dis your key chain?

AKI: Yeah, where you wen' find 'um?

TOMI: Out dere someplace, I dunno where.

(MIKAME *opens the screen door, holding out a small paper bundle.*)

MIKAME: Toshio, take this to the outhouse.

TOSH: What's that?

MIKAME: Present from Otōsan.

TOSH: Aeh, smell like unko.

AKI: Did Otōsan use my portable toilet?

MIKAME: Yes.

TOSH: Well then, let Aki take it.

MIKAME: Toshio, hayō, hayō, busy.

(TOSH *reluctantly takes the bundle and exits.* MIKAME *reenters the house.*)

TOMI: You was wit' Haruko las' night?

AKI: Haruko? Wat she said?

TOMI: She said you taking her to Honolulu.

AKI: I neva said dat. You know, you sista kinna scary. She get all kine ideas in her head, and I dunno where she get 'um from. I neva promise her nuttin'.

TOMI: You wen' sleep wit' her?

AKI: No, no, I promise, I neva do dat. Cross my heart, faddah, muddah die. (*He does so.*)

TOMI: Sometimes Haruko can get little kichigai.

AKI: Well, I not interested in Haruko. She kinna . . . she only tink about herself. Spoiled, yeah.

TOMI: Not her fault. My folks too busy, dey no mo' time for her, so half da time dey dunno wat she doing.

AKI: How come you wen' turn out okay?

TOMI: You dunno dat. Maybe me jus' da same as Haruko.
AKI: No, I been watching you, and I see how you help my folks, especially my old man. You get good heart. I like dat.
TOMI: Wat, you like borrow money from me?
AKI: No, I jus' telling you wat I tink.
TOMI: I betta go back in da house.
AKI: No, try wait. You get boyfriend?
TOMI: No mo' time for da kine.
AKI: You tink you might eva come to Honolulu?
TOMI: I dunno. No mo' reason to go.
AKI: Tomi, our whole family going move to Honolulu fo' sure. You like go too?
TOMI: Me? Wat I going do dere?
AKI: You can stay wit' us and we can pay you to help us, especially wit' da old man. . . . Honolulu good, you know.
TOMI: Wat about Haruko? She like you.
AKI: No, no, she jus' like I take her to Honolulu. She like go real bad. But I guess you know dat by now. She no care about me. She only care about herself. Not like you.
TOMI: Wat I said?
AKI: Tomi, come wit' us. I can ask you parents if okay.
TOMI: I old enough to go any place I like.
AKI: I know my faddah and muddah would be happy.
TOMI: I dunno. I cannot even . . . Haruko would get mad at me.
AKI: I can explain to her if you like.
TOMI: You like I go wit' you folks only to help wit' your faddah? Nuttin' else?
AKI: Well . . . I dunno . . . maybe, ah . . .
TOMI: If I go wit' you, Haruko no going talk to me again. She going tink I like go because I . . . you . . . and . . .

(*She hesitates, then quickly enters the house. Lights fade to black.*)

Scene 5

(*Later in the day.* MIKAME *opens the door as* TOMI *helps* KAZUO *to the rocking chair.*)

KAZUO: Akira helping again?
MIKAME: Yes, he said he needs the exercise.
KAZUO: Tedesuke, no. Work is work. This not a park for fun.

MIKAME: You know Akira. He doesn't want to admit he can work. Now give me your feet. Have to trim your nails.
(MIKAME *sits on the porch and grabs one of his feet. With scissors she slowly trims his toenails.*)
KAZUO: I don't want him working on the farm. Tell him to stop. His work is too sloppy. (*Yelling out to the boys.*) Oi! Oi! Itai! Nani? Watch out, that hurts. My foot is not a cucumber.
MIKAME: Sorry. Your nails are thick and hard. Very stubborn—like you.
KAZUO: Let Tomiko do for me.
MIKAME: No, it's dirty work.
TOMI: I don't mind. I can do it.
KAZUO: Yes, she's better. Not clumsy like you. Itai!
MIKAME: Sorry.
TOMI: Kamiya-san, I'll treat your feet like two hibiscus flowers.
KAZUO: Too bad I don't have a daughter like you to take care of me. Only two boys.
MIKAME: If we had a daughter, she would help me, not you.
KAZUO: No, daughter always has more affection for the father.
MIKAME: Mother and daughter are closer.
KAZUO: Well, too bad you didn't produce a girl.
TOMI: Akira was talking about his older brother who died.
KAZUO: Hmmm. Kishiyo. He was a good boy. Always listened to me. Always followed me and helped me. When I climbed a tree to pick coffee, he would pick up loose coffee berries on the ground. He stayed close to me all the time. He made me very happy.
MIKAME: Kishiyo was a dream boy. Too good to be true. Maybe that's why he was taken from us. He was too good for us.
KAZUO: (*To* TOMI.) He wasn't strong. When he got sick—he was so sick—he said, "Otōsan, I feel bad. Make me better. Otōsan, help me." But I couldn't heal him. All I could do was sit with him and say, "Don't worry, Kishiyo, I'm here with you. I won't leave you."
MIKAME: He stayed with Kishiyo day and night until he died.
KAZUO: I thought it was the end of my world. My boy, Kishiyo.
MIKAME: But we still have Akira and Toshio.
KAZUO: They're nothing compared to Kishiyo.
MIKAME: Don't talk like that.
KAZUO: It's true.
(TOSH *enters with a bag of guavas and hands it to* MIKAME.)
TOSH: I picked the guava you wanted.

MIKAME: Arigatō.
KAZUO: What's that for?
MIKAME: I'm going to make jam for Akira to take with him.
KAZUO: Don't do it! Not for him, the good-for-nothing! Itai!
TOMI: Sorry.
   (*Embarrassed,* TOMI *hands the scissors to* MIKAME *and enters the house.*)
MIKAME: If you stay with Otōsan, I can pick the pohā.
TOSH: No, I'll do it. Then Aki can hoe hana all by himself. He'll like that.
   (*He leaves.*)
KAZUO: Pohā jam, too?
MIKAME: Pohā jelly.
KAZUO: For Akira?
MIKAME: Do you have to ask?
KAZUO: Do what you want. Just don't cut my toenails.
MIKAME: We have liliko'i out there, too. I can make—
KAZUO: Yes, yes, Akira likes liliko'i jelly too.
MIKAME: No, I'll make it for you. That's your favorite, ne?
   (*She smiles at* KAZUO *as lights fade to black.*)

Scene 6

(*The following day, noon. A lighted spot downstage left.* HARUKO *enters the light.*)

HARUKO: I going wit' Aki. Ever'ting going be diff'rent 'cause Aki love me. In Honolulu I no need do laundry work. I can be free and do wat I like.
   (TOMI *enters.*)
TOMI: Haru, Aki no love you.
HARUKO: You jealous.
TOMI: No. I jus' no like you t'row yourself at guys leaving Kona. Shame, you know, everybody talking.
HARUKO: You like Aki for yourself.
TOMI: I no like you get hurt.
HARUKO: Wat you care about me. Betta if I go Honolulu, den you no need see my face.
TOMI: Haru, no talk li'dat. We sistas.
HARUKO: I no care. You trying to take Aki from me.
TOMI: I no like Aki.

HARUKO: No lie. You like marry him. Why else you told Papa you going help take care da Kamiya old man in Honolulu?
TOMI: We can use da money, 's why.
HARUKO: You lie, you lie. Da kine money dey pay you, you can do betta in da canefields or working for da haoles.
TOMI: Be quiet.
HARUKO: Wat kine future we get in Kona? We can marry one tedesuke who no can do nuttin' but hoe da weeds and pick coffee all day. And we can be jus' like Mama, growing old and tired from ovawork wit' one husband who no care for her, who no love her.
TOMI: Stop it, you talking about our parents!
HARUKO: I no care! I hate dem, bot' of dem. All dey know is work, work, work, and da only reason why dey had kids is so we can be slaves for dem and—
(TOMI *grabs* HARUKO *by the arms, shaking her roughly.*)
TOMI: Shut up, shut up, you talking crazy, dey going hear you.
HARUKO: Let 'um hear, I no care. Tell 'um, tell 'um!
(HARUKO *exits, weeping. Lights fade to black.*)

Scene 7

(*Half an hour later.* MIKAME *and* TOSH *come out of the house.*)

MIKAME: Let me see your ears. Kitanai, I know.
TOSH: Not dirty.
MIKAME: Full of mimi-kuso. Come here.
(*He lies next to* MIKAME *and puts his head on her lap, extending his palm to her.* MIKAME *takes out a bobby pin and carefully digs into his ear.*)
Hmmm, see. Mitemi. I was right. . . . If you go to Honolulu, who will clean your ears?
TOSH: You will, Okāsan.
MIKAME: My arms aren't that long.
TOSH: You have to go too. You and Otōsan.
MIKAME: No, I don't think so.
TOSH: You have to, or I won't go. I won't leave you and Otōsan, especially the way he is now.
MIKAME: Kona has been good to us. We have everything we want in Kona. We have friends and a Japanese community. Good Kumamoto people.

TOSH: You think this is the good life because that's all you know.

MIKAME: I know how hard it was in Kumamoto. Families suffered because of bad times. Here, we always have work, food, clothes, a house to sleep in. We have everything we need.

(TOSH sits up.)

TOSH: Yes, we always managed with hard work. But I want to make something more of myself. I want you and Otōsan to be proud of me. That can only happen if I go to Honolulu.

MIKAME: I'm proud of you now. No mother can expect more of a son.

TOSH: Okāsan, you just don't understand how I feel. I hated it when Jiro Sakai went to college. I felt so stupid. I can't look at Jiro or talk to him, I'm so embarrassed.

MIKAME: I'm sorry, but we needed you on the farm. It was our fault—

TOSH: No, I don't blame you.

MIKAME: You want to be like Jiro?

TOSH: It's not that.

MIKAME: You're a much better son than Jiro. I know, because I talk to Sakai-san and she says Jiro is ashamed of her and her husband. It hurts her. She's happy for her son and that it's worth the pain, but.... Are you ashamed of me and Otōsan?

TOSH: No, no. Is that it? Are you afraid I might turn out like Jiro? Is that why you—

MIKAME: No.

TOSH: Because I wouldn't be like him. You and Otōsan mean so much to me. That's why I can't leave you and Otōsan alone here.

MIKAME: Let me see your other ear.

TOSH: Aki is renting a house now. He wants the three of us to join him. But if Otōsan doesn't want to live with Aki, we can find another place. If that would help ... anything, I would do anything.

MIKAME: It's so hard. How can you tell Otōsan to give up his life here? Does he deserve that, after all he's done?

TOSH: Okāsan, what can I do? I feel like I'm dying every day. What's going to happen to me? I'm afraid. I'm afraid I'm going to be left behind, and someday I'll be old and alone on this farm, and everybody will be gone.

(MIKAME *sees* TOSH's *tears. She's not a touchy person, but here she puts her fingers to his face to touch his tears. She can't help but shed tears, too, and wipes away her tears with the towel on her lap.* AKI *has come from around the house and sees what is happening. Lights fade to black.*)

Scene 8

(Ten minutes later. AKI *sits alone on the porch.* HARUKO *enters.)*

HARUKO: Aki, Aki.
    (He hurries to her.)
AKI: Haruko, wat?
HARUKO: Wen you going to Honolulu?
AKI: Why?
HARUKO: 'Cause I gotta get ready.
AKI: Haruko, Tosh and me taking our folks to Honolulu. No mo' room fo' you.
HARUKO: Aki, I love you.
AKI: No, no, 's crazy.
HARUKO: No say dat, I not crazy.
AKI: I mean, I wen' jus' come back few days ago and already you love me? Impossible.
HARUKO: Please, please.
AKI: No mo' place fo' you in my life. Sorry, but, right now I worried about my folks da mos'. You gotta unnastand. Okay? I no like hurt you but—
HARUKO: You love Tomi.
AKI: Tomi? Why you say dat? She said someting?
HARUKO: Tell me if you love her.
KAZUO: *(From inside the house.)* Oi! Oi! Nandai!
AKI: See? My faddah need lotta help. Urusai but no can do nuttin'. I gotta take care him.
HARUKO: Wat I going do? Wat I going do?
AKI: No cry, no cry. Dat no going help. Haruko, someday you can go Honolulu, but not now. You too young. You gotta grow up firs'.
HARUKO: I already eighteen.
AKI: 'S not wat I mean.
    (TOSH *brings out a badly limping* KAZUO *as* MIKAME *holds the door open.* KAZUO *sits in his rocking chair.* TOMI *enters.)*
TOMI: Haru, I wen' hurt you. Sorry. If Aki like take you to—
AKI: No, no, I already explain to her dat—
HARUKO: No pity me. Get plenny guys like take me away. Jiro. Jiro Sakai. He can take me to da mainland if I ask him. Mainland betta. I no need you. If you love Aki dat much, you can go wit' him. Da family not going miss you. Go. I no care. Betta if you go.
TOMI: Haruko, I no like we fight. No blame da folks. Dey trying deir bes'.

HARUKO: For who? Not for me.
TOMI: I no like worry dem. You going be da only daughta wit' dem while I stay in Oʻahu. Dey need you. Mama especially. She worry about you da mos'.
HARUKO: So you like I stay home wit' dem? You stupid, no. I going run away da firs' chance I get. I know you, you like leave here jus' as much as me. Only you no like admit it. You go, go, see if I care.

(HARUKO *backs away and exits.*)

AKI: Sorry.
TOMI: Was bound to happen, soona or later. . . . My folks said okay for me to go wit' you folks.
AKI: You faddah no care?
TOMI: Well, betta I go dan one of da boys. I guess he was mo' worried about dat. Me no problem.
AKI: 'S good. You going be big help.
TOMI: I betta go now. I was worried about Haruko.

(*She exits.*)

MIKAME: What did they want?
AKI: Came to say good-bye. I'll be returning to Oʻahu in a couple of days. Okāsan, it was nice seeing you again. I didn't realize how much I missed you till I got back. Otōsan, good to see you, too. You haven't talked to me since I've been back. You haven't asked what I'm doing in Honolulu or why I'm back. You act like I don't exist. That's fine. I know I hurt you by running off the way I did years ago. I understand how you feel. You expected a good, obedient, hard-working son and I turned out lazy and rebellious, a good-for-nothing who enjoyed having a good time with the bad crowd. . . . Say something. Talk to me. Talk to me, I deserve that much.

(KAZUO *remains silent.* AKI *turns and starts to walk away.*)

KAZUO: So, you finally admit how worthless you are. Bakatade. What good are you as a son?
AKI: I know. Too bad Kishiyo had to die. I was just a little boy, but I still remember how you cried and cried when you held Kishiyo's dead body in your arms.
KAZUO: Don't talk about Kishiyo.
AKI: It would've been better if I had died instead of him. He was such a good son. And I never told you this before, but you were a good father. You worked hard, you made sure we always had food to eat and clothes to wear. I never felt deprived in the material things. So Toshio and I thank you for all that.

TOSH: Yes, Otōsan. You worked the hardest of all the fathers. Now it's time for you to take it easy. We have something to tell you.

AKI: Your legs are bad, and they aren't going to get better.

KAZUO: You don't know, you're not a doctor.

AKI: You can't go out in the fields and hoe hana the way you used to. You're helpless without Toshio. And you can't expect Okāsan to carry you on her back.

KAZUO: Toshio is here. You don't have to stay. Go back to Honolulu. I don't care.

AKI: Toshio wrote me a letter and said he wanted to move to Honolulu, too. He wants to study and learn things he can only learn in the city. He deserves the chance, Otōsan.

(KAZUO *stares at* TOSHIO, *who can't look him in the eye.*)

You understand, don't you? Toshio has been the good son I never was. But he's young and smart, and he can make something of himself. He can be more than a farmer. I believe in him. You know that, too. You know Toshio is special. He can make you proud.

TOSH: Otōsan, my dream is to become a builder. I'm good with my hands. I'll work as a carpenter in Honolulu, go to school until I'm smart enough to build homes for people. I want to be as good as the haole builders.

KAZUO: (*To* MIKAME.) Tell them. Tell them it's impossible.

AKI: We want to sell the lease to the farm and take you and Okāsan to Honolulu to live.

KAZUO: Baka! I won't go. I'll die on this land first.

AKI: Don't you understand, we want to take care of you. I'll make sure you won't have to worry about anything again.

KAZUO: I don't want your help. All these years I didn't need you and I don't need you now.

AKI: Yes, you do. For once in your life you need me, and this time I'm here for you. But you have to go to Honolulu.

KAZUO: Never.

AKI: What can you do in Kona, on this farm? What can you do? You stubborn old man, wake up, wake up and see what you are—a poor, crippled, dirt-poor farmer who—

MIKAME: Akira, stop, enough!

AKI: No, Okāsan, he has to hear. I got you now, Otōsan; you can't walk away from me. You have to sit and listen.

(KAZUO *tries to get up to walk away. He lurches and is about to fall.*)

MIKAME: Abunai!
(TOSH *grabs* KAZUO *and puts him back in his chair.*)
AKI: You see, you see. You're a weak, helpless old man. You have to go with us.
KAZUO: My legs will get better.
AKI: No, your legs are useless.
KAZUO: Toshio, tell him.
TOSH: Aki's right. Your legs are not going to get better. The doctor said so. I'm sorry.
(KAZUO *looks to* MIKAME, *who keeps silent.*)
AKI: Yes, I'm taking you with me, even if I have to pack you on my back like a baby.
KAZUO: I have to stay. I must work to make the money I need. . . . I promised I would . . .
AKI: Promise what? Who?
KAZUO: You can't understand. No, no. No, no, no.
TOSH: Aki, wait. Otōsan, you want me to stay, I'll stay. I'll stay with you and Okāsan in Kona.
AKI: (*Pulling* TOSH *away.*) No, Tosh! You no see wat he doing? No give in to him now. No let him get his way again.
TOSH: But, Aki, wat I can do?
AKI: I no going let you t'row away your life. You get one good future ahead of you; no let him block you, no let him destroy your life. Otōsan, see what you're doing to Toshio! You want him to sacrifice his life for you? Why? You had your chance in life. Don't deprive Toshio of his. You're a selfish, arrogant old man, always thinking only about yourself. Is that how your mother raised you? What kind of mother was she? Selfish and arrogant like you? She was a witch, mean and hateful, and I'm glad I never knew her.
(KAZUO *suddenly rises and reaches out to strike* AKI, *but he falls to the ground.* TOSH *moves to help, but* AKI *holds him back.*)
You're a hopeless cripple. Your time has past. It's gone. Now it's Toshio's chance.
(KAZUO, *weak and frustrated, crawls pitifully on his side, reaching out to grab* AKI *by the ankle. He tries to pull* AKI *down, trying, trying, but it's no use. He sobs, his shoulders quivering, his body curled up, like a baby.* MIKAME *sits next to* KAZUO, *stroking his arm gently.*)
Otōsan, you see, I'm stronger than you. And I'm doing what I think is best for all of us, the way you did what was best for us when we were

children. I already asked Tomi Ishitani to go with us, and she said yes. She'll be a big help. Toshio and I won't let you down. You'll see. I'm not the same person who left here six years ago. I've changed. I'm sorry I hurt you, but I know what I'm doing is right.

MIKAME: Let's go with them. Ne? Your boys worry about you, they love you. When we are young, the children follow us. When we get old, we must follow the children. Ne?

(AKI *walks away to stage left, then slowly sinks to the ground with his legs folded and head bowed.* MIKAME *continues to stroke* KAZUO's *arm as the lights fade to black.*)

Scene 9

(*Later that day, evening.* AKI *is now lying on the ground, a lighted lantern nearby.* SHOGO *backs out of the house, bowing.*)

SHOGO: Okusan, oishii, oishii, gottsōsama, gottsōsama.
(*He turns to join* AKI.)
Aki, I almos' no can believe you folks all moving to Oʻahu. Oh, going be lonesome.

AKI: (*Sitting up.*) Shogo, why you no come wit' us? You can stay in my house too.

SHOGO: Me? Hmmm, you always had good heart, Aki. You always nice to me. You jus' like you faddah.

AKI: I dunno about dat. So come wit' us. No need worry about nuttin'. I help you find one job too. Maybe you can work at da nursery wit' me.

SHOGO: Arigatō, but I gotta stay in Kona.

AKI: Why? You no mo' family o' nuttin'; we go.

SHOGO: No can. Da obake lady wen' tell me to stay here.

AKI: Da obake? She in her undawear again?

SHOGO: No. But she wen' talk to me fo' da firs' time.

AKI: Yeah? Wat she said?

SHOGO: She said to stay in Kona, work hard, save my money, and someday I going own my own land and get rich.

AKI: Good, Shogo, good. I hope so fo' your sake.
(TOSH *comes out of the house to join them.*)

TOSH: You ask Shogo already?

AKI: He like stay in Kona.

SHOGO: You tink da Okazaki family can use me too?

TOSH: Sure. I tell 'um you one hard worka.
SHOGO: T'anks, eh, Tosh. I going miss everybody wen you go. Why everybody gotta leave. Firs' my faddah, den my muddah, now you folks.
AKI: Go get married, Shogo, raise you own family.
SHOGO: Yeah, no. You tink Haruko Ishitani like me?
AKI: Shogo, you can do betta dan her.
SHOGO: Maybe I can get one wife from Japan.
AKI: No. Japanese no can come into da country to live anymo'. Pau. 'S da law.
SHOGO: Hontō? Since wen?
AKI: Few years ago. So you no can bring back one Japan wife. How 'bout one local girl?
SHOGO: Well, mos' local Japanee girls, wen dey see me coming, dey run away. I wonda why?
TOSH: Dey no mo' brains, 's why. Dey dunno you would make one good husband.
SHOGO: How 'bout Kanaka girls? Wat you tink? Dey nice and dey no run away from me.
AKI: Aeh, you live in Hawai'i, why not marry one Hawaiian.
TOSH: Yeah, Shogo, no worry about dat.
SHOGO: Maybe I betta ask you muddah. She smart.
AKI: She da' bes. Go ask.
  (SHOGO *trots back into the house.*)
  So how's da old man?
TOSH: Good ting you wen' invite Tomi fo' dinna. She know how to talk to da old man. She said all da right tings. I tink da old man feel betta because Tomi coming wit' us. You no hungry? You like I bring you someting?
AKI: Nah. Bumbai. I feel funny staying in da house. I tink I going sleep outside tonight—wit' da stars.
TOSH: I getting nervous about moving.
AKI: Aeh, you gotta do good. Show da old man not one mistake go to Honolulu. Everyting depend on you now. Gambare, eh. Give 'um all you get.
TOSH: T'anks, Aki. I no going fo'get wat you did fo' me.
  (TOMI *emerges from the house.*)
AKI: Nah, nuttin'. I owe you dat much fo' staying wit' da folks all dis time, and fo' being one good son. I gotta go back, but wen da time come to move, I come back help. No worry.

TOMI: I tought I betta come out 'cause Shogo getting all excited about getting one wife. I wonda how come he get da kine idea all of a sudden?
AKI: One cockaroach wen' whispa in his ear.
TOMI: Your muddah telling him all kine stuff.
TOSH: I gotta hear dis.
   (*He jogs back to the house.*)
TOMI: Maybe you should tell your muddah find you one wife, too.
AKI: Me? Yeah, if I can find one girl jus' like my muddah. . . . Wat about you? You like marry one guy like Jiro?
TOMI: No. Da guy ack real high tone, yeah. He tink he one haole or someting. I no like one stuck shit like him.
AKI: Tomi, you going like it in Honolulu. I going make sure a dat.
   (*The soft lantern glow is warm and soothing.* AKI *puts a hand lightly on her shoulder. She smiles, takes his hand, and places it on his lap. Soon lights fade to black.*)

THE END

MĀNOA VALLEY

MĀNOA VALLEY

Time: The summer of 1959, the year of statehood.

Place: The backyard of the Kamiya home in Mānoa Valley.

Scenery: The exterior of a large white house with a screen door. Service porch with steps leads to a cement patio. Decorating the area are a picnic table, two benches, a round table with some chairs, and pots of flowers. One walkway leads offstage right to an unseen nursery area. Another walkway heads off upstage left around the house. The third walkway is downstage left leading to the front of the house.

CHARACTERS

TOSH KAMIYA, *head of the household, a nisei, age fifty*
FUMIKO KAMIYA, TOSH's *nisei wife, forty-nine*
LAURA, *their daughter, twenty-five*
SPENCER, *their son, nineteen*
DEBBIE, *their youngest daughter, thirteen*
UNCLE AKI, TOSH's *older brother, fifty-five*
AUNTIE TOMI, AKI's *wife, fifty-three*
NOBU, *their son, twenty-six*
SUSAN, NOBU's *white wife, twenty-four*
TOKU TANIGUCHI, LAURA's *husband, twenty-six*

ACT ONE

(*It is midmorning. There is the chirping of a bird.* TOSH *comes out of the house in a white undershirt and striped boxer shorts. He wears rubber slippers on the porch and walks downstage to the cement patio. He looks up at the sky and surveys the area with the look of a contented man.*)

TOSH: Mama! Mama!
FUMIKO: (*At porch.*) Wat happen?
TOSH: Try come.
   (FUMIKO *goes to him, concerned. She wears a simple shirt and slacks. Her hair is covered by a scarf.*)
   Try look. Da rain wen' away. Going be one nice day for da party.
FUMIKO: You call me out jus' for dat? I tought someting was wrong wit' you. No make me scared for nuttin', eh.
TOSH: You sure get enough kau kau for today?
FUMIKO: Of course.
TOSH: Shame, you know, if no mo' enough food.
FUMIKO: No worry, we can feed one army. Wassamadda you.
TOSH: I like da party be extra special. Not every day we going celebrate statehood. Can you imagine, Hawai'i da fiftieth state. About time, yeah. No mo' second-class citizenship now.
FUMIKO: Yeah, but we still so far away from da mainland.
TOSH: We no need worry about dat. Today, no need worry about nuttin'.
FUMIKO: Well, if you happy Hawai'i is one state, den I happy, too. But I no mo' time talk to you. I gotta cook, clean da house, Laura gotta fix my hair...
TOSH: Territory was not enough. And I neva like commonwealth. Had to be statehood. 'S da bes' way. Some guys neva like believe me, but I know I was right.
DEBBIE: (*From inside the house.*) Mama!
FUMIKO: Out here!
   (DEBBIE *comes out to the porch.*)
DEBBIE: Mama, where my... Daddy, you in your underwear.
   (TOSH *looks at himself.*)
TOSH: So?
DEBBIE: Da neighbors get one free show, man.
TOSH: Oh yeah? Go charge dem one dollar.
FUMIKO: Da neighbors no can see. Go wake up Spenca.

Mānoa Valley

DEBBIE: Dat sleepy head. You gotta hit him wit' one shovel to wake 'um up.
TOSH: Go, go. Tell your bruddah I said no can sleep late today.
DEBBIE: Okay, but I going bring one baseball bat wit' me.
(DEBBIE *reenters the house.*)
TOSH: Mama, someday I like build one house on dis side. (*Indicates the area over the audience.*) For Spenca, wen he get married. Wat you tink?
FUMIKO: Get plenty room.
TOSH: Might as well make use, eh.
FUMIKO: Yeah, you can make one nice house dere.
TOSH: Sure. If Spenca get t'ree, four kids, he need one big house. So ova dere jus' like he living wit' us even though not in da same house.
FUMIKO: You get everyting all figured out, eh.
TOSH: I was looking at all dis space we get. I dunno. Maybe haoles might put tennis court or someting, but I tink betta if we build someting for our son.
FUMIKO: I hope Spenca appreciate it.
TOSH: Oh yeah. Wen Spenca graduate from University of Hawai'i, he can work full time wit' me, den take ova da business someday. Den his son take ova for him. Jus' like da Dillinghams, eh, on and on. Da Kamiya and Son Corporation. How you like dat?
FUMIKO: You sure know how dream big.
TOSH: Why not? Now dat Hawai'i is one state, no telling how good business going be. No kidding. 'S why I told Spenca take business administration at UH. Den he can handle da books.
FUMIKO: You work too hard; you gotta take it easy, listen to da doctor. Wen you retire, den—
TOSH: Wen I retire, I still going keep track of da business. No can jus' play every day. Eva since I was one small kid, I was working. If I no work, waste time.
FUMIKO: I wish Spenca wasn't so lazy.
TOSH: Nemmine. Da important ting now is dat he study hard at school, get his education. Not like me. How long I hadda go night school jus' to get my high school diploma.
FUMIKO: No can help; you had to quit school wen you was young to help your folks pick coffee.
TOSH: Yeah, 's why I no like Spenca suffa for nuttin'. So long as he get good grades, I no care about da odda stuff. He going work wit' his head, not his hands.
FUMIKO: You gotta be more strict wit' him, like your faddah was wit' you.

TOSH: No, I strict enough. I not going make da same mistake like my faddah. He was one tough old man, too tough. Aki neva can stand him wen he was young. So wat my bruddah did? Run off to Honolulu. No, I not going chase Spenca away from da business. I going make 'um easy for him. Dat way he can make one good life for himself wit' da business and build 'um some more afta I ma-ke.

FUMIKO: Aeh, no talk about dying yet. Afta you retire, I going take you to Japan, mainland, Europe. You undastand wat I saying?

TOSH: Okay, okay.

(SPENCER *comes out in a T-shirt and swimming shorts. His hair is disheveled.*)

SPENCER: Mama, where my breakfast?

FUMIKO: You nebosuke, tell your sista cook for you.

SPENCER: You like she poison me or wat?

DEBBIE: (*Behind him.*) Yeah, no give me ideas.

(*She hands* TOSH *a pair of pants. She is also carrying a small camera.*)

TOSH: Wat dis for?

DEBBIE: Daddy, you look betta wit' your pants on. Your legs too white. Look like shark bait.

FUMIKO: Yeah, Daddy, you getting old. Now you gotta listen to your daughter.

TOSH: (*Putting on pants.*) Ya-re, ya-re.

(FUMIKO *and* SPENCER *exit into the house.*)

DEBBIE: Daddy.

(*She snaps a picture of* TOSH *still with his pants down.*)

TOSH: Aeh, wat you doing?

DEBBIE: Blackmail!

(*Elvis the dog barks offstage right.*) Hi, Elvis!

TOSH: Tell him shut up.

(*She exits. The barking soon stops.* FUMIKO *comes out.*)

FUMIKO: Daddy, da mush going be ready quick so come in already.

TOSH: Same old ting every morning. Quaka Oats. Me not one horse, you know.

FUMIKO: Mush is good for you.

TOSH: How 'bout Portogee sausage and eggs sunnyside up?

FUMIKO: Too strong. You not one kid anymore.

(*She reenters the house as* DEBBIE *returns.*)

DEBBIE: Elvis' chain was tangled up. Daddy, you know wat I was tinking?

(TOSH *doesn't answer. He is deep in thought, looking out where* SPENCER's *future house is going to be.*)

Daddy.

TOSH: Huh?

DEBBIE: Wat you tinking?

TOSH: Oh, I was tinking I get one good business, good wife, good children. Wat more I like?

DEBBIE: Good Portogee sausage and eggs.

TOSH: Yeah, but your muddah is strict.

DEBBIE: She worry about you; she not trying to be mean.

TOSH: I know. 'S why I said I get one good wife.

DEBBIE: You tink me one good daughter?

TOSH: Well, you get good grades in school. You listen to Mama, you help around da house. Wat else?

DEBBIE: 'S about it. But you neva tell da bad side. I spend too much on records and clothes. I go see too many movies, and next week I gotta start wearing braces on my teeth. 'S too expensive, so I betta not put da braces on. Instead, I like save da money for college.

TOSH: No worry. I get enough money for college and your teeth.

DEBBIE: Daddy, you work too hard for your money. I can go wit'out da braces.

TOSH: Wat Mama going say?

DEBBIE: You know Mama, she going say I need da braces, but she always worry about small tings like dat.

TOSH: No, you get da braces so you get nice, straight teeth, not like mine. See how funny? 'S because my muddah and faddah was too poor to fix my teeth for me. But you, you going get teeth like one princess.

DEBBIE: Yeah but princesses no need braces; dey born wit' good teeth. No fair, man.

(SPENCER *comes out to the porch.*)

SPENCER: Mama said come in before da mush get cold.

TOSH: Okay, okay. You finish already?

SPENCER: Yup.

TOSH: Wat you wen' eat?

SPENCER: Same old ting. Portogee sausage and eggs.

(TOSH *shakes his head as he exits into the house. The dog barks again.*)

SPENCER: Shut up, Elvis!

(*The dog doesn't stop.*)

Dammit!

(SPENCER *runs off in his bare feet.* FUMIKO *comes out.*)

FUMIKO: Spenca, hurry up, eh.

SPENCER: (*Offstage.*) Damn dog crazy.

DEBBIE: Mama, I tink Elvis like find his girlfriend.

(SPENCER *returns.*)

SPENCER: I like take off his chain and let 'um run loose.
FUMIKO: No, bumbai he run in odda people's yards.
DEBBIE: You no feel sorry for him, all tied up?
FUMIKO: Only one dog, nemmine. Spenca, I told you go get da chairs and bring 'um outside. Hurry up.
SPENCER: Nobody here yet, for wat rush?
FUMIKO: Nonkena, no you. How you going do anyting? Be more like Daddy.
SPENCER: Daddy is Daddy, me is me.
FUMIKO: Wat you mean by dat?
SPENCER: No two rivers run da same way. Da Mississippi go dis way, da Nile dat way.
FUMIKO: You like I show you which way to go?
SPENCER: I going, I going.

(SPENCER *goes into the house.*)

FUMIKO: Dis for you. Peel da cucumbers please.

(*She hands a bowl of cucumbers with a peeler to* DEBBIE.)

DEBBIE: (*Peeling at picnic table.*) How many people coming to da party?
FUMIKO: About forty. Da boys from work, business friends. Das why we wen' make all da laulau last night.
DEBBIE: You ain't kidding, man. My fingers still tired. But why we making one party for statehood?
FUMIKO: You know your daddy. He like celebrate for da new state.
DEBBIE: He get funny kine ideas sometimes.
FUMIKO: You be quiet, no say nuttin' to Daddy.

(SPENCER *comes out carrying three beach-type chairs in both hands. He places them around the patio.*)

SPENCER: One chair was rip, so I neva bring 'um out.
FUMIKO: I told you fix da chair long time ago.
SPENCER: I was busy.
FUMIKO: Busy, busy, always busy. Here, make yourself useful. Clean da tables and benches.

(*She gives him a rag, then exits into the house.*)

DEBBIE: You lazy bone.
SPENCER: Quiet, shrimp, before I clean you wit' dis rag.

(*The dog barks again.*)

Dat did it.

(*He exits.* DEBBIE *watches and reacts to what she has seen. He returns.*)

DEBBIE: Now you going get it. Why you let Elvis loose for?
SPENCER: If he like go, let 'um go. Not natural keep him tied up like dat. (*He cleans the tables.*)
DEBBIE: I hope he don't make da Chandlers' dog pregnant.
SPENCER: Wat you know about pregnant?
DEBBIE: Enough.
SPENCER: No make me laugh.
DEBBIE: You know da Higashi lady, da one Mama talks to at da store sometimes?
SPENCER: Yeah.
DEBBIE: Well, her daughter got pregnant.
SPENCER: Who told you dat?
DEBBIE: I heard Mama and Daddy talking. Anyway, da girl neva say nuttin' to her muddah for long time.
SPENCER: Dat was stupid.
DEBBIE: I know. Wen her faddah found out, he wanted to kick her out of da house.
SPENCER: 'S wat she get, keep her mout' shut so long. She should've told her muddah right way. Dumb.
DEBBIE: Well . . . you told Mama yet?
SPENCER: Tell her wat?
DEBBIE: You know. About you.
SPENCER: Me? I not pregnant.
DEBBIE: I mean, dat you like go to mainland school.
SPENCER: (*Pauses.*) Wat happen to da Higashi girl?
DEBBIE: She getting married and dey moving in wit' her folks.
SPENCER: Her folks?
DEBBIE: Yeah, da boy's faddah wen' kick him out of his house first.
SPENCER: All's well dat ends well in da land of aloha.
DEBBIE: Why you have to go to mainland school for?
SPENCER: You no feel isolated living on one small island in da middle of da ocean?
DEBBIE: No.
SPENCER: Every morning I wake up, I feel like da whole world running way ahead of me and I no can catch up. I get up ten A.M., already one P.M. in L.A. and four o'clock in New York. Everyting happening in da world and I still sleeping. You know wat I mean?
DEBBIE: No.
SPENCER: You jus' one girl, you no can undastand.

DEBBIE: Well, get up seven A.M., den only ten o'clock in L.A. and one P.M. in New York. Not so bad den.
SPENCER: I get itchy feet; I gotta go.
DEBBIE: Maybe you jus' get athlete's foot.
(FUMIKO *is out with a mop.*)
SPENCER: Mama, I like talk to you.
FUMIKO: Wat?
SPENCER: Try come.
FUMIKO: Wassamadda now.
SPENCER: No get excited now, but I—
FUMIKO: Wat? Wat you did? You bang da car again?
SPENCER: No, nuttin' like dat. I wen' apply to go to USC.
FUMIKO: USC? Mainland?
SPENCER: Yeah, and dey accepted me.
FUMIKO: Wat about UH?
SPENCER: I can transfer my credits from dere.
FUMIKO: But why you have to go to business school ova dere?
SPENCER: Not for business, Mama. I like study someting else.
FUMIKO: You have to study business, so you can take ova for Daddy someday.
SPENCER: 'S da whole point, Mama. I no like take ova da business.
FUMIKO: Why?
SPENCER: Da business not mine.
FUMIKO: Of course 's yours. Daddy said he going—
SPENCER: I know wat Daddy said. I know wat he always say, but 's his business, going always be his business. Wen he die, going still be his business. Da rest of my life he going be telling me wat to do and how to do it. I cannot be a building contractor.
FUMIKO: How hard you tink Daddy working so you can go school. He depending on you.
SPENCER: I gotta be my own boss.
FUMIKO: Baka. I no like hear da kine stupid talk. No hurt Daddy for nuttin'.
SPENCER: I know. 'S why I tought maybe you can tell him.
FUMIKO: No. Daddy stay plan everyting out and—
SPENCER: But Mama . . .
FUMIKO: Wait little while and tink some more. Den you can see wat I mean. No spoil today for Daddy.
(LAURA *enters from downstage left. She's wearing a shirt and slacks. Her head is covered with a scarf, and she's carrying a muumuu in a plastic hanger bag.*)

LAURA: Hi, everybody.
DEBBIE: Hi, Laura.
LAURA: Mama, you like I make your hair right away?
FUMIKO: Well, if not too much trouble.
LAURA: No, we go in da house.
DEBBIE: Where Toku?
LAURA: He coming. You know how slow him. Toku! Spenca, how come you neva cut your hair?
SPENCER: Why, what's wrong?
LAURA: You look like one hoodlum. Mama, you going let him stay like dat?
FUMIKO: I get enough tell him anyting.
   (TOKU *enters carrying a large box. He wears an aloha shirt with gray trousers and rubber slippers.*)
TOKU: Oh, hi!
   (*He playfully tries to dodge* SPENCER.)
LAURA: Watch out, no drop da box.
DEBBIE: Toku, wat happen to your hair?
   (TOKU *sports an obviously new haircut that is fairly short and poorly cut. A cowlick sticks out in the back part of his head.*)
LAURA: Nuttin' wrong wit' his hair.
DEBBIE: But he had da nice Waikīkī wave in front wit' da long sideburns.
TOKU: No mo' now.
LAURA: Swept away in da garbage can.
DEBBIE: Da mean barber you had. He wen' crazy, yeah.
LAURA: Looks nice. Cheap, too.
DEBBIE: Who did it, Toku?
TOKU: Laura.
LAURA: Was real easy. Spenca, come inside. I cut your hair too.
SPENCER: You gotta catch me first.
LAURA: Mama, next time you go cut your hair, I can do 'um for you.
FUMIKO: Well, I tink I going let 'um grow little bit.
   (TOKU, LAURA *and* FUMIKO *enter the house.*)
DEBBIE: Toku sure must love Laura a lot to let her cut his hair like dat.
SPENCER: Toku is too nice guy. Someday he gotta tell Laura who da real driver of da car.
DEBBIE: Laura always let Toku drive. She's a good side-seat driva. Go dis way, Toku, go dat way. No, you going da wrong way.
SPENCER: Debbie, wen you grow up, no be like Laura.
DEBBIE: Why?
SPENCER: You promise?

DEBBIE: Why?

SPENCER: 'Cause I like you stay young—and stupid.

DEBBIE: You moe lepo.

SPENCER: If anybody like me, tell 'um I fixing my car.

DEBBIE: Again?

SPENCER: Yeah. I need time to tink. And around here da only time I can tink is wen I fixing my car.

(SPENCER *exits left as* TOKU *reappears.*)

TOKU: Dey keeping you busy, eh.

DEBBIE: Yeah, I hate da parties at dis house. I gotta do all da dirty work.

TOKU: Wat you making?

DEBBIE: I peeling da cucumbers for da namasu. All I do is peel dis, peel dat. Mama don't know it, but she preparing me for my future career.

TOKU: Yeah? Wat dat?

DEBBIE: One burlesque stripper. I so good at peeling dat I decided I going peel off my clothes for a living.

TOKU: No kidding. Wat you going call yourself?

DEBBIE: I dunno. How 'bout Madame Pele, da Goddess of Volcanic Passion?

TOKU: Sound interesting. I can come see da show?

DEBBIE: All relatives and in-laws cannot see da show. Only strangers, sad-faced men wit' empty eyes.

TOKU: Where you going dance?

DEBBIE: Beretania Follies. 'S one clean place?

TOKU: No ask me. I neva go dere in my life.

DEBBIE: Toku, I heard you telling Spenca once about wat you saw.

TOKU: Wen?

DEBBIE: We was picking seaweed last year and you was wit'—

TOKU: You was dat far away and you heard?

DEBBIE: I hear everyting within a one-mile radius.

TOKU: I gotta watch out for you, you get X-ray ears.

DEBBIE: No worry, Toku, I not going tell Laura.

TOKU: (*A friendly wink.*) T'anks, eh.

(LAURA *steps out with a preserves jar and a bowl of carrots, giving the jar to* TOKU *and the bowl to* DEBBIE.)

LAURA: Open dis. Peel da carrots, Debbie. I hope Uncle Aki dem don't come too soon.

DEBBIE: Why?

LAURA: 'Cause my hair not ready. I no like Susan see me like dis.
(TOKU *can't open the jar.*)
Toku, no get your clothes dirty out here. I like you look nice wen Nobu and Susan dem come. Debbie, watch him, eh, no let him do someting silly. You know him. Wassamadda, you dat weak?
TOKU: Really tight.
LAURA: Here, Daddy can open 'um. He getting da poker room ready.
(*She reenters the house.*)
DEBBIE: Da cova was probably rusted inside.
TOKU: No, was jus' tight.
DEBBIE: You know wat I tink?
TOKU: No, wat?
DEBBIE: I tink Laura need one baby.
TOKU: You tink Laura can make one good muddah?
DEBBIE: Well, she like boss people around, jus' like my muddah. If she get one baby, she can boss da baby around.
TOKU: I dunno. I tink betta if we no get kids, too much trouble.
DEBBIE: Toku, I heard you and Laura talking, and you said you wanted kids. Laura, too.
TOKU: Wen you heard dat?
DEBBIE: Wen you, Laura, and me went to Kapiolani Drive-in to see *Jailhouse Rock*.
TOKU: Yeah? Chee, dat was . . . I tought you was sleeping in da back seat?
DEBBIE: I was. But I still heard.
TOKU: You and your X-ray ears.
DEBBIE: 'S how I learn about life, Toku. Nobody tell me nuttin'. You know, if I get married, I going be jus' like Mama and Laura. I tink I going boss my husband around. And I going hate myself because of dat, but still I not going change.
TOKU: How old you now?
DEBBIE: Thirteen and a half.
TOKU: Going on tirty-five.
(TOSH *comes out.*)
TOSH: Aeh, Toku, put your head down. Now side to side.
(*Yelling into the house.*)
Laura, I going keep my barber.
(LAURA *emerges with a handful of gobō wrapped in newspaper.*)
LAURA: 'S up to you, Daddy. I willing to do it for you.

TOSH: Well, I been going to da same guy for ten years now, no use change, eh. Bumbai he feel bad.
LAURA: Debbie, you so slow, wat you doing?
DEBBIE: I only get two hands, you know.
LAURA: Here, do da gobō too.
DEBBIE: I will neva, eva, be a vegetarian.
TOSH: Toku, you wen' bring money for da poker game?
TOKU: Yeah, and I going win back wat I lost last time.
LAURA: Daddy, no make Toku lose so much.
TOSH: Wat you like I do, cheat for him?
LAURA: If you have to, yes.
   (FUMIKO *comes out.*)
TOKU: Going be diff'rent today. I feel lucky.
LAURA: You always feel lucky and you always come home wit' your pockets empty.
TOKU: Not every time.
LAURA: We not rich, you know.
FUMIKO: Toku, you ate breakfast yet?
TOKU: Yeah, I cook my own today.
LAURA: He cook his breakfast every morning now, Mama. I get him trained real good.
FUMIKO: Shame on you. You neva used to be lazy like dat before.
TOKU: Nah, 's okay. No trouble.
FUMIKO: For wat you wen' study home economics at UH?
LAURA: No ask me. I was tinking maybe I going back to school and take some courses.
TOSH: Nemmine dat. You gotta raise kids firs'. Yeah, Mama. Den you can send your kids to college.
LAURA: I get enough wit' one big kid here.
TOSH: No blame Toku. Next year is good time to get one baby. 1960 is wat, Mama? Year of da horse? Someting good like dat, yeah?
FUMIKO: I tink year of da rat.
LAURA: See! No baby next year.
TOSH: No listen to Mama; she dunno nuttin' about Japanese calendar.
   (*He makes a face at* FUMIKO.)
FUMIKO: Next year is year of da rat.
TOSH: You dunno how lie or wat?
   (*The phone rings in the house.*)
TOSH: 'S for me. Hanapi supposed to call.
   (*He enters the house.*)

FUMIKO: Oh, Toku, t'anks for da big Samoan crab. Where you wen' catch 'um?
TOKU: Inside Kaneohe Marine Base.
FUMIKO: And da Hawaiian crabs, about twenty.
TOKU: 'S nuttin'. Me and my friends wen' catch about sixty crabs. We jus' t'row out da crab nets wit da aku heads as bait, wait little while, den pull 'um up. You should see da crabs in da nets—sometimes t'ree, four in one catch.
LAURA: Mama, if I let him, he go fishing and crabbing every day.
TOKU: Good fun das why. We drive down dis narrow dirt road. Get only enough room for one car, and we gotta twist and turn past bushes and trees. Nobody around but us. Really quiet and peaceful. Now on one side get big fishing ponds and bushes. On da odda side is da bay, and in da distance across da bay, we can see da jets taking off and landing.
TOSH: (*From inside.*) Mama, try come!
FUMIKO: Now wat?
(*She goes in.*)
DEBBIE: Anybody can go in da marine base?
TOKU: Yeah. If you folks like go, I can get passes for everybody.
(LAURA *busies herself on the porch.*)
One ting we do, wen we catch crabs full wit' eggs, we always t'row 'um back in da ponds. Gotta give 'um chance to reproduce. You take care of da land, da land take care of you.
DEBBIE: I bet you can live off da land, I mean, all da time.
TOKU: Yeah. Dat was my life. No need worry about nuttin'. Do wat I like wen I like.
DEBBIE: But den you wen' marry Laura.
TOKU: Yeah. You know why?
DEBBIE: No, why?
TOKU: I tell you in five years.
(*Elvis barks offstage right, then the barking moves across to offstage left.*)
LAURA: Aeh, how come Elvis running loose? Go catch him, Toku; everybody else busy.
TOKU: Okay. Elvis my friend.
(*He exits left.*)
DEBBIE: Why you let Toku go afta Elvis?
LAURA: Why not?
DEBBIE: 'S not his dog. Anyway Spenca wen' untie him. Let him chase Elvis.

LAURA: Spenca? Nineteen years old and he still ack like one kid. Daddy baby him too much.... I take da cucumbers and carrots inside. No forget da gobō.

(LAURA *enters the house.*)

AKI: (*Offstage left.*) Oi! Oi! (*He enters with a clucking chicken in a cardboard box with holes.*) Hi, Debbie, where Mama?

DEBBIE: Hi, Uncle Aki. She in da kitchen.

AKI: You like dis chicken?

DEBBIE: Chee, how come you wen' bring one live one?

AKI: Here, you take 'um.

DEBBIE: Uh-uh, I ain't no country girl.

(AKI *laughs heartily.*)

Going get one cockfight or wat?

AKI: No, we going eat dis chicken.

DEBBIE: We going eat one live chicken?

AKI: 'S da bes' kine. Fresh. But firs' we gotta (*He zips his forefinger across his throat.*) kreee!

DEBBIE: Yuck!

AKI: Fumi! Oi, Fumiko!

(FUMIKO *at the door.*) Chicken, chicken, bring da knife. I going be waiting by da tree stump.

FUMIKO: Okay.

(*She withdraws as* AKI *exits right.* NOBU, *toting a baby bag, enters with* SUSAN, *who's carrying an infant in a bundle.*)

NOBU: Aeh, Debbie, how's my favorite cousin?

DEBBIE: Hi, Nobu! Oh, you brought the baby. Hi, Susan.

SUSAN: Hello, Debbie, nice to see you again.

(TOMI *enters carrying a bag of malasadas.*)

DEBBIE: Hi, Auntie Tomi!

TOMI: Mo' and mo' big, eh, you.

DEBBIE: Chee, Auntie, you only saw me last month.

(FUMIKO *comes out with a large, menacing knife and waves it in the air.*)

FUMIKO: Nobu! Oh, good you came.

NOBU: Thanks for inviting us.

TOMI: Watch out da knife, eh, no cut off your fingers.

DEBBIE: Mama, look da baby.

AKI: (*Offstage.*) C'mon, Fumi!

FUMIKO: Susan, thank you for coming. How's little Daniel?

SUSAN: I hope you don't mind that we brought him.

FUMIKO: Of course not. Oh, he's so cute. Hello, Daniel.
NOBU: Daniel Akira Mason Kamiya.
DEBBIE: He get two middle names?
SUSAN: Mason is my father's name.
FUMIKO: (*To* TOMI.) Fast, no. Yonsei already.
SUSAN: Yonsei?
NOBU: Fourth generation AJA.
SUSAN: AJA?
NOBU: American of Japanese ancestry.
AKI: (*Offstage.*) Fumi, wat you doing? Dis chicken giving me da stink eye!
TOMI: Shut up, you! (*She starts to exit offstage.*) Dat old man get big voice for nuttin'.
FUMIKO: (*Calling into the house.*) Laura, boil some water. Nobu, come, go in da house, da front way. Relax in da parlor. Come, Susan, I take you inside.
NOBU: Don't worry about us, Auntie. You busy right now. I wanna show Susan out here, anyway.
FUMIKO: Oh, okay. Debbie, tell Daddy hurry up and come outside and show Susan and Nobu around.
NOBU: No, don't bother him. He must be busy.
FUMIKO: He jus' changing his clothes. Take him one whole day to decide wat to wear, jus' like one wahine.
AKI: (*Offstage.*) Fumi, dis chicken going die of old age!
FUMIKO: Okay!
DEBBIE: Mama, wat you gonna do with that knife?
FUMIKO: I going chop off da chicken head, of course.
DEBBIE: You?

(FUMIKO *exits. The chicken squawks loudly. There is the loud thud of the knife on the stump.* DEBBIE *and* SUSAN *wince.*)

DEBBIE: You think that hurt?
SUSAN: I hope not.

(FUMIKO *enters, wiping the knife with a cloth.* TOMI *walks beside her. They go to the picnic table, where* TOMI *places a bag of malasadas.*)

TOMI: I wen' bring some malasadas. Dey jus' make 'um.
FUMIKO: You didn't have to.
TOMI: You busy in da kitchen?
FUMIKO: Yeah, we get lotta work for you. You can roll da sushi.
TOMI: Okay, good. Susan, I take Daniel inside.
SUSAN: All right.

TOMI: Baby not hungry yet?
SUSAN: No, he's resting pretty good. Maybe later.
  (*She hands the bundle to* TOMI. FUMIKO *carries the bag of malasadas.*)
TOMI: C'mon, Aki-chan, grandma take you in da house.
FUMIKO: Debbie, stay here wit' Nobu and Susan till Daddy come.
DEBBIE: Okay.
  (FUMIKO *and* TOMI *enter the house.*)
DEBBIE: By the way, did you see Elvis out front?
SUSAN: Elvis? Elvis Presley?
DEBBIE: No, Elvis Kamiya, our dog.
SUSAN: (*Smiling.*) Oh . . .
NOBU: He barked at us coming up the walk.
DEBBIE: How 'bout Toku?
NOBU: No, he didn't bark at us.
DEBBIE: Nobu . . .
SUSAN: He was trying to catch Elvis, but he slipped in a mud puddle.
DEBBIE: Poor Toku.
  (FUMIKO *carries out a deep pot of hot water.*)
FUMIKO: Uncle still trying to decide wat to wear.
NOBU: Let me help you, Auntie.
FUMIKO: No, you get nice clothes on.
DEBBIE: What's that for, Mama?
FUMIKO: We going clean off da chicken feathers.
  (*She exits.*)
DEBBIE: I don't know what you gonna make with that chicken, but I ain't eating it! I'm not eating that chicken, are you?
SUSAN: Well, I don't know.
DEBBIE: Susan's not eating the chicken too!
SUSAN: No, I didn't say that. Ah, chicken's fine with me!
NOBU: Come on, Debbie, it's only a chicken.
DEBBIE: I know, but I saw that chicken when it was alive. Now . . . I'm gonna check out what they're doing.
  (DEBBIE *exits.*)
SUSAN: It's beautiful here. So lush and green and clean.
NOBU: Mānoa has lots of rain and rainbows.
DEBBIE: (*Offstage.*) Uncle! Aaaeeeehhhh!
NOBU: It hasn't been so bad, huh?
SUSAN: No, just a little different—from Michigan, I mean. But I expected that.

NOBU: Things'll get better. You'll never regret coming back to Hawai'i with me.
SUSAN: Oh, I know that.
NOBU: Miss your family?
SUSAN: Well, I hope someday Dad understands about us.
NOBU: Sure he will. Look, if you want, take Daniel back for a visit. When your father sees him, he'll change his mind about us getting married.
SUSAN: I don't know.
NOBU: He can ignore me, but he can't deny his own grandson, even if he is half Japanese. Danny's so cute, your father won't be able to resist him.
SUSAN: His first grandchild, after all.
NOBU: Of course.
TOMI: (*Offstage.*) Look out! No make a mess!
AKI: (*Offstage.*) Yakamashii!
NOBU: My mother couldn't be happier with Danny.
SUSAN: And me? Is your mom happy with me?
NOBU: Sure. . . . She hasn't said anything, has she?
SUSAN: No.
NOBU: Well, maybe she had her heart set on me marrying some Japanese from Hawai'i; that's understandable.
SUSAN: It's okay that we're not going to live with your folks?
NOBU: Perfectly okay.
SUSAN: I don't want to cause problems, but . . .
NOBU: It's fine, believe me.
SUSAN: I'd just feel better if I didn't have someone looking over my shoulder all the time.
NOBU: I know. Mom's used to being boss around the house, that's all. She lives by the old ways. Well, she has to learn.
SUSAN: I don't want her to hate me.
NOBU: Don't be silly. She's not that kind of person, anyway. Hey listen, you like this place?
SUSAN: Yes.
NOBU: Okay, one day I'm gonna build a bigger and better home for you.
SUSAN: When I'm old and gray?
NOBU: Oh no. We're going places, baby. And fast. I can see our shiny new house, maybe up on Tantalus overlooking the city. Or past Diamond Head with the sea at our doorstep. A magnificent castle for my fairy-tale princess.

SUSAN: My chivalrous knight on a charging white steed with banners flying.
(*They kiss.* SPENCER *enters from left, wiping his hands with a rag. He looks around to see that no one else is around.*)
SPENCER: Ah, Nobu, I can ask you something?
(*They break off the kiss.*)
NOBU: Yeah, yeah, Spenca. What's up?
SPENCER: You know, when you told Uncle Aki you were going to the mainland for school, what did he say?
NOBU: Chee, that was a long time ago. Let me think. Ah, he said something like, "Make sure da haoles no take you cheap. If dey ack smart, give 'um one."
SPENCER: He wasn't mad at you?
NOBU: What for?
SPENCER: Well, you know, that you were leaving Hawai'i and all that.
NOBU: No. But you know my father—he couldn't care less about what I do.
SUSAN: That's not true. He cares a lot about you. He just doesn't express it verbally.
NOBU: Sure, sure. Anyway, why the concern, Spenca?
SPENCER: Oh, ah, I don't know. I mean, he didn't say you couldn't go?
NOBU: No. But I was awarded a scholarship, so . . .
SPENCER: If he tried to stop you, what would you have done?
NOBU: I don't know. Never thought about it.
SPENCER: What if he said you had to stay home and take over his nursery?
NOBU: The nursery? Oh, no, no. That's his life. My goal was to become an attorney. He knew that. Things change. We progress. We go on to better things. For me to grow, I had to go to the mainland, to stretch my imagination, to spread my wings of adventure. It's my life, after all, right?
SPENCER: Yeah, yeah, right. Thanks.
(SPENCER *goes to the porch, searching for a tool.* DEBBIE *races in.*)
DEBBIE: You wanna smell something really bad? Go over there and put your nose over the chicken and feathers in the hot water. Phew!
NOBU: Yeah, let's go.
SUSAN: No thank you.
NOBU: Reminds me of my childhood. I remember the family went to Kona for a visit. It's a real country place, and the people there killed a chicken for dinner. It was supposed to be a real treat.
SUSAN: Well, you go and relive your childhood. I'll stay here with Debbie.
NOBU: Okay, but you're missing one of the joys in life.

DEBBIE: Better hold your nose

(*He smiles and pinches his nose as he exits.*)

FUMIKO: (*Offstage.*) Spenca, no forget da tub and ice.

SPENCER: Okay.

(*He exits with a screwdriver.*)

DEBBIE: Do you want something to drink? Soda?

SUSAN: No thank you.

DEBBIE: Something stronger, maybe? Vodka Collins? Bloody Mary? My father has a bar inside. I can mix any drink you want.

SUSAN: It's too early for me. Maybe tonight.

DEBBIE: Okay.

SUSAN: Who taught you to mix drinks?

DEBBIE: Nobody. I taught myself. I try to learn everything I can. If times get hard, I can always be a bartender.

(LAURA *comes out in a colorful muumuu, hair neatly coiffed.*)

LAURA: Susan!

SUSAN: Hi, Laura.

LAURA: Oh, you look so nice. Where'd you buy that?

SUSAN: A shop in Waikīkī. On Kala . . . Kala? . . .

LAURA: Kalākaua Avenue. Isn't it expensive there? It's for the tourists. I'll take you to the stores where the local people shop.

SUSAN: Oh, good, that'll be nice. You have a lovely place here.

LAURA: Oh, I live in Kaimukī; it's not as nice there. Debbie, you didn't finish the gobō.

DEBBIE: Well, I was busy talking—

LAURA: Don't make excuses. I gotta do it myself.

SUSAN: Can I help?

LAURA: Oh no, you're a guest here.

SUSAN: No, please, I want to.

LAURA: Well, okay.

SUSAN: Maybe I can work on the . . . gobō?

(TOKU *enters with his soiled pants rolled up.*)

LAURA: What happen?

TOKU: Nuttin'.

LAURA: Look at your pants. Now you gotta go home and change.

TOKU: Not going take me dat long.

LAURA: Put that pants in the laundry sink and wear the blue gabardine in the closet.

(NOBU *and* FUMIKO *enter.*)

NOBU: Hi, Laura.

LAURA: Nobu, aeh, you look shaka today.
NOBU: Auntie, what kind of chicken you making?
FUMIKO: Heka.
NOBU: Good. You make the best chicken heka.
   (FUMIKO *smiles and exits into the house.*)
SUSAN: How'd the chicken smell?
NOBU: Great! Smelled as bad as when I was a kid. Some things never change.
LAURA: Let's go in the house. By the way, is Nobu a kid like Toku?
SUSAN: Nobu? Oh, worse.
TOKU: I guess I betta go before she spank me, eh, Debbie?
   (TOKU *exits.* TOSH *finally emerges in neat trousers and a drab aloha shirt.*)
TOSH: Nobu!
NOBU: Aeh, Uncle, howzit?
TOSH: Susan, you look jus' like one local girl in your muumuu. Terrific.
SUSAN: Thank you, Tosh. You look terrific too.
TOSH: Dis shirt not too flashy? Oh, where you going?
SUSAN: Inside. I'm going to help.
TOSH: No, no, come, come, I have to show you outside.
   (LAURA *exits with a friendly shrug.*)
   Aeh, Aki, you like one beer?
AKI: (*Offstage.*) Only if you get Primo!
TOSH: Debbie, get Uncle one beer. You like one, Nobu?
NOBU: Not right now.
   (DEBBIE *exits.* TOSH *scrutinizes* NOBU.)
TOSH: Nobu, how come you still tuck in your shirt like one haole?
NOBU: Yeah, I gotta buy some aloha shirts.
SUSAN: What about those at home?
NOBU: Oh no, that's from high school days. My mother just didn't throw them away. (*To* TOSH.) You know Mama, eh, she never throws anything away.
TOSH: Yeah, if you poor wen you young, you like save everyting wen you get old.
   (DEBBIE *brings out a beer in one hand; with the other she pinches her nose as she exits right.*)
   I hear you moving outta da house? How come, get plenty room at home.
NOBU: Yeah, but now that we get Daniel, too noisy for the folks.
SUSAN: Daniel cries a lot. It's natural at his age, but still . . .
   (DEBBIE *returns.*)

Mānoa Valley

NOBU: Anyway, we'll visit the folks all the time. They gotta babysit their grandson sometimes too.
SUSAN: We'll always keep in touch. It's not as if we're moving to Alaska.
NOBU: Sure, it's not a far drive to Kalihi.
TOSH: Yeah, yeah, you right.
TOMI: (*At the door.*) Debbie, come help. No be lazy.
DEBBIE: Me help? Help wat? I ain't peeling nuttin', man.
TOMI: Yeah, you peel da potatoes. Hayō, Mama like you.
DEBBIE: (*Exiting.*) Peel, peel, peel, aaaaaagggghhhhhh!
NOBU: The law firm I'm joining is downtown, so we're renting a house in Nu'uanu.
SUSAN: It'll be a couple of weeks before we move in.
NOBU: Susan's going to teach at Punahou this year.
TOSH: Too good, eh. 'S one high-class school, you know.
SUSAN: I'll just be a substitute teacher, but I'm looking forward to it.
(*SPENCER enters with an aluminum tub and a bag of ice.*)
TOSH: Spenca went to a private boys school—'Iolani. Debbie going to a girls school—Saint Andrew's Priory. Only Laura went to a public school—McKinley. Afta Spenca graduate from UH, he going work full time wit' me in da business.
(*SPENCER looks up but decides against speaking.*)
NOBU: What's that for, Spenca, the beer?
SPENCER: Yeah, the guys from work can suck 'um up.
TOSH: Summertime Spenca helping me, but he get plenty to learn.
NOBU: At least you're there to teach him.
TOSH: He learning da bes' way—from da bottom up.
DEBBIE: (*At the door.*) Spenca, Mama said get the charcoal grill.
SPENCER: Get 'um yourself.
TOSH: Aeh! Go!
SPENCER: Why I gotta do all the slave labor?
TOSH: Wat? Not going kill you. Help Mama today, you know she busy.
SPENCER: I sick and tired of doing everything around here—and at work.
TOSH: Work? Wat you doing at work? You get one easy job helping da working men.
SPENCER: Yeah, all the dirty work.
TOSH: Wat dirty work?
SPENCER: Picking up all the trash at construction sites.
TOSH: 'S good for you. Teach you to keep da area clean and safe so nobody get hurt.

SPENCER: I don't have to learn that.

TOSH: You like do wat I did wen I was one kid? I hadda climb up stepladdas and pick coffee berries till my legs shaking and my arms like fall off. From morning till night. You tink you like dat?

SPENCER: Better than what I doing now.

FUMIKO: (*At the door.*) Spenca. Get da charcoal grill ready. Hayō!

(SPENCER *reluctantly exits.*)

TOSH: Kids nowdays, I dunno.

NOBU: Growing pains.

(FUMIKO *goes back in.*)

TOSH: Nobu, I hope you hungry. Going get plenty 'ōno kau kau today.

NOBU: Oh, I'm ready. The one thing I missed on the mainland was Hawaiian food.

SUSAN: What was 'ōno kau kau again?

NOBU: Delicious food.

SUSAN: I'm trying to learn all the new words I hear.

TOSH: You going catch on real fast. Get one haole girl in Waikīkī working for one U-drive company. She can talk Pidgin betta dan me. And she only been here two years.

NOBU: I don't think Susan wants to learn Pidgin, Uncle. She's an English teacher.

TOSH: Oh, den I betta watch out how I talk to you. In dis house we speak combination English, Hawaiian, Japanese. Real chop suey.

SUSAN: Sometimes I don't understand what Tomi is saying.

NOBU: I told Mama to watch how she talks with Susan, but . . .

TOSH: Hard for your muddah, eh, she talk like dat for so long.

SUSAN: No, honey, I want to learn, so it's better if I hear it all the time. It's an interesting dialect.

TOSH: Come, let me show you da hothouse.

SUSAN: What kind of plants does Fumiko grow?

TOSH: Fumiko? 'S not her hothouse. 'S mine. I grow nuttin' but orchids. Cattleya, Vanda, you name 'um, I got 'um.

(*As they exit,* SPENCER *enters with a portable grill.* DEBBIE *joins him from the house.*)

DEBBIE: Why you got mad at me for? Not my fault.

SPENCER: I not mad at you. I jus' gotta go to da mainland. Gotta settle dis damn ting today.

DEBBIE: Wat about Daddy?

(AKI *enters with the deep pot.*)

AKI: Debbie, you like see da chicken now? Nice and clean, no feathers.
DEBBIE: No t'anks. I not going look at anodda chicken as long as I live.
  (AKI *exits into the house, laughing.*)
FUMIKO: (*From inside.*) Debbie!
DEBBIE: I know! Peel da oranges!
  (DEBBIE *races inside.* SPENCER *drops the grill and exits.* AKI *reemerges with several knives and a sharpening stone.*)
AKI: Ho, da junk knifes you get.
FUMIKO: (*From inside.*) No can help, nobody make 'um sharp for me.
AKI: I fix 'um up, going be sharp like one samurai sword.
  (TOMI *comes out and busies herself on the porch.*)
TOMI: No ack so smart, eh, bumbai you cut off your da kine.
AKI: Good. Den you no bodda me in bed.
TOMI: Aeh, quiet, eh, you. Debbie can hear.
AKI: So? If she dunno about da kine stuff, she betta find out before too late. 'S right, eh, Debbie?
TOMI: You drunk or wat?
  (DEBBIE *comes out.*)
DEBBIE: You call me, Uncle?
AKI: Oh. Ah, you heard me wat I said jus' now?
DEBBIE: About wat?
AKI: About, ah, you know, da kine stuff.
DEBBIE: Wat kine stuff?
AKI: You still one kid yet, no.
DEBBIE: Well, I still going school.
AKI: Yeah, yeah, wat dey teach you?
DEBBIE: Science, history, math, English. Stuff like dat.
AKI: Dey no teach you da odda stuff?
DEBBIE: Wat odda stuff?
AKI: You know . . . da kine.
DEBBIE: Wat kine?
TOMI: Aki!
AKI: 'S okay.
DEBBIE: Uncle, you going tell me or wat?
AKI: No, bumbai you auntie konk me on da head. Go back help in da kitchen.
TOMI: Yeah, 's good training for you wen you get married.
DEBBIE: I neva getting married.
TOMI: Why?

DEBBIE: 'Cause I no like get pregnant.
AKI: Wat? You know about da kine?
DEBBIE: Yeah, why?
AKI: I like you go teach Auntie; she dunno nuttin'.
DEBBIE: Oh, Uncle, you always kidding.
AKI: Who kidding?
>   (DEBBIE *enters the house.*)
>   (*To* TOMI.) See! (*He decides to sit on the cement now.*)

TOMI: Aeh, watch out your pants, eh.
AKI: Nemmine my pants. If I like puka pants, 's my business.
>   (SPENCER *enters with another tub and a case of beer.*)
>   Spenca, I tell you one ting. No eva get married.

TOMI: No listen to your uncle. He drink two beers and already he drunk.
AKI: Aeh, I can drink ten beers and I still talk mo' sense dan you. Spenca, you eva see me drunk?
SPENCER: Chee, Uncle, ah, you know . . .
TOMI: No ask Spenca lie for you.
AKI: Wat you mean, lie? Spenca, listen to dis. (*He winks at* SPENCER, *making sure* TOMI *can't see.*) Put your hand ova your heart. Okay now. You tell da trut', da whole trut' and nuttin' but da trut'.
SPENCER: Yes, sir.
AKI: Did you eva, in your whole life, see me, your favorite uncle, who is a real sharp guy, get drunk?
SPENCER: Well, at Laura's wedding, you—
AKI: Wait, wait. You need eyeglasses or someting?
SPENCER: No, my eyes good.
AKI: Okay den, wait. (*He surreptitiously pulls a dollar bill from his pants and flashes it to* SPENCER, *making sure* TOMI *doesn't see. He points to the bill, then to* SPENCER.) How your eyes now?
SPENCER: Perfect.
AKI: Now we cooking. Did you eva—
SPENCER: No, Uncle, I neva saw you drunk in my life.
AKI: Case dismiss!
>   (TOMI *shakes her head and exits into the house.* AKI *resumes his work, spitting on the stone and scraping a knife on it.*)

SPENCER: Here, Uncle. (*Holding out the dollar.*)
AKI: Huh? No, no, 's yours.
SPENCER: I no need.
AKI: Nemmine. I not happy unless I broke ass. Where your Daddy?

SPENCER: Showing Nobu and Susan da hothouse.
AKI: Mo' betta your Daddy was da nurseryman instead of me. . . . You know I was one professional gambla wen I was young? Your Daddy eva tell you dat?
SPENCER: No, he no talk about da old days to me.
AKI: Yeah, I was one real rascal. And I was happy, too. But I wen' make one big mistake in my life. You know wat dat was?
SPENCER: You had pair jacks and you wen' try bluff one guy who had royal flush.
AKI: Worse dan dat. I wen' marry your auntie. Not dat your auntie dat bad, but if I neva marry her, I can stay one bachelor. You see—
SPENCER: Yeah, but if you neva get married, den you no get Nobu and Nobu no get Daniel and—
AKI: Aeh, who telling dis story, you or me?

(LAURA *comes out with a tray of coffee cups.*)

LAURA: Uncle, you like coffee?
AKI: Who made 'um?
LAURA: Auntie Tomi.
AKI: You like I drink my wife's coffee? You pupule or wat?
LAURA: Why, wassamadda?
AKI: Taste like shellac. Spence can drink mine.
LAURA: You like?
SPENCER: Not afta wat Uncle said.
AKI: You smart.

(TOSH, SUSAN, *and* NOBU *return.*)

NOBU: For a while I was thinking about staying on the mainland, but there's lots of things to do in Hawai'i.
TOSH: Good you came back. Make your muddah happy.
LAURA: I have coffee for you folks, and don't ask who made it.

(*They sip their coffee.*)

TOSH: Aaaaaggghh, Auntie Tomi made dis. Taste like shellac.
LAURA: You and Uncle just the same. No wonder you're brothers.

(*They put the cups back.*)

TOSH: Aki, no shame, eh. Drink up, get plenty beer.
AKI: Yeah, no worry.
SPENCER: Here, Uncle. (*He hands a bottle to* AKI.)
TOSH: Yeah, your muddah was real happy wen you wrote you was coming home. Too good da way you wen' study on da mainland.
NOBU: Going to Michigan was the best thing I could've done.

SPENCER: Nobu, I bet you learned things on the mainland you could never learn in Hawai'i, right?
NOBU: Oh, yeah. One thing I learned is you gotta get along with the haoles. You know, on the whole, they were really nice to me on the mainland. Especially this haole.
SUSAN: Don't think I don't know who you mean. (*To* TOSH.) I just felt sorry for him.
NOBU: I had to watch how I talked. Sometimes the Pidgin came out. Hard to talk. Everybody thought I was shy, but I was too embarrassed to say anything. Until I met Susan.
SUSAN: He's just fooling. Nobu was never shy. He was always campaigning, advocating causes, getting people involved. I loved the way he took charge of things. He wouldn't take no for an answer.
AKI: He get dat from his muddah.
SPENCER: What if you never went to the mainland? What if you were stuck here all this time?
NOBU: Boy, I hate to think about that.
SUSAN: If you didn't get the scholarships, you'd be working in the nursery now.
NOBU: Maybe. Or be a hoodlum.
SUSAN: Hoodlum?
NOBU: Honey, I came from Farrington; that's a tough school.
TOSH: Once he got suspended for fighting.
NOBU: (*To* SUSAN.) I took on two guys.
SUSAN: Yet sometimes he's so quiet I don't know whether he's listening to me or sleeping.
AKI: He learn dat from me. I pull dat on my wife all da time. Jus' last night.
SUSAN: But you were really sleeping.
(AKI *shakes his head.*)
NOBU: Like father, like son.
SUSAN: Oh, you. Next time I want your attention, I'll dump a pitcher of water on you.
AKI: No tell my wife your plan. I can jus' see her creeping up on me and . . .
(*He mimes dumping a pitcher and shivers.*)
SUSAN: Mum's the word.
TOSH: Let's go to da odda side of da house. I pick you some mangoes. Wen we firs' moved here, Aki and Nobu helped me plant da trees. Right, Nobu?
NOBU: Yeah, those trees really grew.

TOSH: Still giving fruit.
(*The three exit upstage left.* LAURA *sips coffee and grimaces.*)
LAURA: Auntie put someting in dis coffee?
AKI: Yeah, go look in her purse. She get 'um wrapped up in tissue paper.
LAURA: Wat is it?
AKI: 'S her secret. If you find out, tell me. I pay you five dollars.
(LAURA *smiles and exits into the house.*)
Your auntie going little bit senile, you know dat?
SPENCER: Wat happen?
AKI: She mix anyting wit' da food. I no can eat wat I like.
SPENCER: Sounds like she and Mama wen' talk it ova.
AKI: She even put barley in wit' my white rice. No 'ōno. 'S why I like come here and eat. At leas' your muddah no do dat.
SPENCER: Auntie neva feed you like dat before, eh?
AKI: No. Started about wen Nobu got married. Funny, yeah. Now she tell me every time, "I no like you die early, 's why I feeding you like dis. If you die now, who going take care of me, who I going stay wit'? I no like live by myself." You know, wen she talk like dat, I no can say nuttin'. Firs', I gotta get married for make my muddah happy. Now I gotta live long to keep my wife happy. I tell you, Spenca, life not so easy. Especially for one rascal like me. Now your faddah was always one good boy, da baby of da family. But he always work hard. 'S why he get plenty money now and one good business, so you can take ova someday. Yeah, you really lucky.
SPENCER: 'S wat I hear all da time. But you neva expect Nobu take ova da nursery, eh?
AKI: Nah. His dreams was bigga dan dat.
SPENCER: 'S wat I mean. Den why I gotta take ova my faddah's business?
AKI: 'S diff'rent. Your faddah get one good business. For wat t'row 'um away. Pohō.
SPENCER: Wat you going do wit' your nursery wen you retire?
AKI: Me? Maybe sell 'um. If I get four, five sons, maybe one of dem like da nursery. But I get only one boy, so no can help. Yeah, was too hard on your auntie, so we stop wit' one kid. You know, maybe I can find one boy like learn da business. 'S wat wen' happen to me. Dis old Japanee man said he no mo' son to continue his nursery, so he going teach me everyting if I work wit' him, and wen he die, he going give me da whole works. He was old already, and he neva get relatives in Hawai'i or Japan. He was one sad old man. He used to like drink, so I used to

get drunk wit' him. And I dunno how many times he used to tell me about his wife in Japan. Wen he was one young man, he wen' leave his pregnant wife and came to Hawai'i to earn some money. He was going back to Japan, but his wife wen' die in childbirt'. Da baby too. So he neva wen' back. He blame himself dat his wife wen' die. Afta dat I guess he put all his energy into his nursery. And I tink he was breaking his back for his wife and kid till da day he died. Yeah, people funny. If dey work hard to build up someting, dey no like da damn ting broke up afta dey ma-ke. Rich people feel like dat, but poor people feel da same way. 'S why dis old man, Nakamura-san, afta he teach me all he know, he kick off, keel ova right in da hibiscus bush, his fav'rite place in da whole nursery. Anshin shita, you know dat word? Anshin.

SPENCER: Kinda. I tink Babasan used to use dat word.

AKI: Babasan? Yeah, I guess so. At leas' you wen' learn some Japanese from your grandmuddah, eh. Anshin, free from care, be at peace. 'S wat dis old man had. He was ready to join his wife and kid. Only one favor he wen' ask me before he ma-ke. Scatta his ashes around da hibiscus bushes. 'S why you see all hibiscus I get.

SPENCER: No tell me you wen' actually scatta his ashes?

AKI: Sure. 'S da old man's spirit ova dere making 'um grow like-a hell. Da old man wen' die long time ago, but he still busting his ass in da nursery. Maybe 's wat I going do, too. I going tell my wife put my ashes around my white plumeria tree. Afta I die, you can come visit me dere. And anytime you need one flowa lei, you can come pick my plumerias.

SPENCER: No t'anks, Uncle. I no like wear no spooky lei.

(LAURA, FUMIKO, *and* TOMI *come out, sipping coffee*.)

FUMIKO: Hot, hot, hot.

TOMI: How long you going take sharp da knifes?

AKI: Pau already. Fumi, watch out wen you use 'um, eh, sharp like-a hell.

FUMIKO: Hai, dōmo arigatō.

AKI: I take 'um in da house, wash 'um for you.

(AKI *exits. The women sit at the picnic table at a distance from* SPENCER, *who is now cleaning the grill*.)

FUMIKO: Erai, erai.

LAURA: Tired, Mama?

(*She massages* FUMIKO's *shoulders lightly*.)

TOMI: Lucky no, you get one good daughta.

FUMIKO: Why, you get one good boy like Nobu.

TOMI: Nah, boys not da same. Gotta be daughta. Too bad I neva get girls like you.

FUMIKO: Well, now you get one nice daughta-in-law.
TOMI: No joke, eh.
LAURA: Auntie, Susan really nice. I like her. Nobu lucky he wen' find her.
FUMIKO: Jus' be grateful Susan and Nobu click wit' each odda.
LAURA: Yeah, and you get one hapa-haole grandson, too good, eh you.
TOMI: But now dey no like live at da house. Get plenty room, no need move out.
LAURA: Auntie, I bet you wen' make bulldog face at Susan, so now she scared of you.
TOMI: No, I always smile at her like dis.
(*She flashes a silly, idiotic, cockeyed smile. They all laugh.* FUMIKO *playfully slaps* TOMI's *arm.*)
FUMIKO: No live wit' da parents, 's haole style. Shōganai.
LAURA: Yeah, no can help. 'S progress.
TOMI: I get one daughta-in-law, but I lose one son.
FUMIKO: Not dat bad. Rememba wen Nobu wanted to marry da Sunada girl?
TOMI: Sunada? Oh, dat girl. All she know was how to spend money. Da faddah sure wen' spoil her. She had her own car, wat was? Buick, I tink. I used to get mad wen she drive up and toot da horn for Nobu. I argue wit' Nobu about dat girl, and Aki always pretending he sleeping. Make me so mad. I used to kick Aki in da leg so he say someting, and all he can say in front of Nobu was, "Why you kick me for?"
LAURA: I rememba her. She was one year olda dan Nobu.
TOMI: She was one freshman at UH. Nobu was fooling around too much wit' her, so I ask your daddy to talk to him.
LAURA: Yeah? Wat he told Nobu?
TOMI: I dunno, but Nobu wen' listen, 'cause afta dat he neva see da girl too much. And den he wen' to college on da mainland.
FUMIKO: 'S why Daddy feel close to Nobu.
LAURA: Wat happen to da girl?
TOMI: Oh, she wen' marry one dentist. I tink he wen' make false teeth for her and fall in love wit' her hagamuge face.
(*She mugs as if she has no teeth with her mouth wide open.* LAURA *and* FUMIKO *laugh at her antics.*)
LAURA: You lie, Auntie, she neva get false teeth. You terrible.
DEBBIE: (*At the door.*) Where Susan? I tink Daniel hungry.
LAURA: She wit' Daddy by da mango trees.
DEBBIE: Okay.
(*She withdraws.*)

TOMI: Susan feed da kid from one baby bottle. I told her breast milk betta, but she said, no, baby formula mo' healthful. Wat you going do?
LAURA: Well, Auntie, 's her baby.
TOMI: Yeah, you betta hurry up and make one kid, too, so your muddah can be one grandmuddah.
FUMIKO: I wonda wat kine grandchild I going get?
LAURA: Wat you folks talking. Get plenty time yet. No need rush.
TOMI: Aeh, no wait too long, eh, going be harda on you, you know.
LAURA: No worry.
FUMIKO: I rememba how happy my muddah was wen you was born.
TOMI: You lucky Laura was one easy baby. (*To* LAURA.) I almost wen' die wen I give birt' to Nobu. I had to get Caesarean. He like stay inside me and no come out. Now, he no can wait to get out of da house.
(DEBBIE *runs out to the porch. Right behind is* AKI.)
DEBBIE: Uncle eating da tempura in da kitchen.
TOMI: Go kick his 'ōkole.
AKI: I only tasting to see if good.
FUMIKO: Well?
AKI: I gotta eat five or six befo' I can give you my opinion.
TOMI: 'S for da party, not for one hoito like you.
AKI: Hoito? Aeh, I work hard sharp da knifes, make me hungry. I like try some sushi too.
FUMIKO: Debbie, cut Uncle some sushi.
AKI: Nemmine, I can cut my own.
(*He withdraws.*)
SPENCER: Aeh, Debbie, bring me some sushi too.
DEBBIE: Come cut 'um yourself.
TOMI: Wat about da baby?
DEBBIE: I warming up da formula for Susan.
(DEBBIE *withdraws.* FUMIKO *checks on* SPENCER. TOSH, LAURA, *and* NOBU *return with a box of fruit;* NOBU *places it on the ground.*)
FUMIKO: You neva finish cleaning da barbecue yet? Guzuguzu no you.
SPENCER: Da grill was rusty. Gotta clean 'um wit' da steel wool. Take time.
NOBU: Chee, Uncle, I don't know how we're going to eat all this fruit.
TOSH: We no can eat all by ourselves. Eat up, eat up.
FUMIKO: Get enough charcoal?
SPENCER: Yeah, but I gotta find da lighta fluid.
TOSH: Da Hayden mango da bes', yeah. Especially if you bite 'um wit' your mouth.

NOBU: Yeah, really sweet and juicy.
SUSAN: And messy. I'm going to wash my hands and check on Daniel.
(*She exits into the house.* TOSH *and* NOBU *join* TOMI *and* LAURA.)
SPENCER: Mama, wait. I gotta tell Daddy today.
FUMIKO: No be silly. Bad time now.
NOBU: Uncle, what would you say if someday I run for politics?
TOSH: I say run fas' so you no lose.
LAURA: What office?
NOBU: Congress. Not right now, of course. I want to put in some time as a lawyer. But when the time is right, maybe try first for the state senate.
TOSH: You really serious, eh?
NOBU: Yes. I have to plan my future. The stakes are high.
TOSH: I give you credit. You cannot be scared. Fumi, try come.
FUMIKO: I talking to Spenca.
TOSH: I like you listen to Nobu. Come. You too, Spenca.
(*As they are joining the group,* TOKU *enters.*)
LAURA: How come you wearing da khaki pants? You no shame? Nobody wears khaki pants to a party.
TOKU: Dis comfortable.
TOSH: Nemmine, leave him alone. Khaki pants okay. If good enough for da Army, good enough for here.
LAURA: Oh, Daddy, no say dat. You only encourage him to act nonki.
(DEBBIE *and* SUSAN *come out to the porch.*)
DEBBIE: Saint Andrew's is a good school, but I have to wear a uniform.
TOMI: Debbie, wat Uncle doing?
DEBBIE: He's in the parlor watching Daniel and television.
SUSAN: The wrestling matches are on.
TOMI: Who wrestling?
DEBBIE: Lucky Simunovich.
TOMI: Ooohhh.
(*She quickly takes her cup and starts to go.* TOSH *stops her.*)
TOSH: Okay now, everybody listen to Nobu.
NOBU: Well, I was telling Uncle that I'm going into politics someday, so I'm active right now at the grass-roots level. It's important to know what people are thinking, and I was at this Democratic meeting and we—
TOSH: Democrat? Aeh, wait. I tought you was one Republican like me?
NOBU: Uncle, the Republican Party is for the Big Five and the rich people in Kāhala. The Democratic Party is for working folks like us.

TOSH: I dunno. I vote Republican all da time. Betta for businessmen. No forget I get one business.

NOBU: Uncle, the post-statehood economy is going to skyrocket. If you think the tourist industry is good now, just wait. We're going to have tourists coming out of our ears. More mainland money coming in, more construction, more jobs, the economic boom is going to get bigger and better.

LAURA: Toku, we gotta start our own business, then you don't have to repair washing machines for McCully Appliance.

TOKU: I like working for somebody else. You no get ulcers dat way.

LAURA: And you can't make money working for somebody, either.

TOKU: Money not everyting.

LAURA: That's not what you say when we have to pay the apartment rent. We can't live only on the fish and crabs you catch.

TOSH: Aeh, okay, okay, let Nobu continue. Important wat he saying.

NOBU: (*Clears throat.*) Politics, that's where we have to make our mark.

SUSAN: That's the only reason why Nobu wanted to return to Hawai'i, to get into politics.

NOBU: Well, not the only reason.

SUSAN: That's what you told me.

TOSH: Tomi, you lucky you get one smart son like Nobu.

TOMI: I dunno. Only smart talk, maybe.

SUSAN: I think Nobu would make a great U.S. senator. You should see how hard he's working, meeting people, making contacts.

NOBU: We can't stand around waiting for other people to tell us what to do. We've got to do it ourselves. Starting from now, 1959, the year of statehood, we have to strive hard to show the other forty-nine states what it means to live in Hawai'i. I want our people to be proud, to stand up straight and look the rest of the world in the eye and say, "We're the best! Hawai'i no ka oi!" We can do it. We will make things happen, we will grow and prosper and lead the way for the rest of the nation. We're going to make Hawai'i the best state in the Union.
(*The gathering applauds.*)

TOSH: Spenca, you hear dat? Study hard like Nobu.

SPENCER: I know. I like study the way Nobu did.

TOSH: Good dat way. Wen you graduate from UH, you can—

SPENCER: I mean, I wanna go to the mainland and study like Nobu.

FUMIKO: Not now.

TOSH: Mainland? Wat wrong wit' UH?

Mānoa Valley

SPENCER: They don't teach what I wanna learn.
TOSH: You know wat he talking about?
FUMIKO: He only told me today.
SPENCER: USC get aerospace engineering.
TOSH: Aerospace engineering? Wat dat?
SPENCER: You study things like orbital mechanics, aircraft structural analysis, flight stability, and—
TOSH: Wat dat get to do wit' business?
SPENCER: Nuttin'.
TOSH: 'S wat I tought.
NOBU: You sure that's what you want, Spenca?
SPENCER: You understand, right, Nobu? (*To* TOSH.) 'S why Nobu went to Michigan. In order to go to law school, he had to study on the mainland. Well, I gotta go to the mainland if I wanna be an aerospace engineer. I applied to USC and they accepted me. I can start in September.
LAURA: USC? In Los Angeles? You cannot go, too expensive. Don't ask Daddy to pay for all that.
TOSH: No, no, wait. I not tinking about da money, but . . .
SPENCER: I pay you back someday. Wen I start working, I pay you back every penny.
TOSH: I neva raise you so you can pay me back.
FUMIKO: Can you get one job in Hawaiʻi as one aerospace engineer?
SPENCER: No, I gotta live on the mainland to work.
TOMI: Wat about Hawaiʻi? You no like come back here?
SPENCER: Cannot help. If no jobs here, then I gotta live on the mainland.
TOMI: Mo' betta stay in Hawaiʻi and run your Daddy's business.
SPENCER: Why? Nobu not going take over Uncle's nursery.
SUSAN: If Spencer wants a career of his own, don't you think he should pursue it, like you?
NOBU: Well, our cases are different. Uncle Tosh has a good contractor business. Who's going to take over when he retires?
SUSAN: Well, I . . .
LAURA: Daddy, if Spenca wants to go, let him. Toku can continue the business.
TOSH: Toku?
TOKU: Me?
TOSH: Toku dunno nuttin' about da business.
LAURA: He can learn.
TOKU: Nah, too hard.

LAURA: You can.

TOSH: No, Toku too nice guy to run da company. You gotta be tough orda da working men around.

LAURA: Then I can be the boss.

TOSH: You? No be silly.

LAURA: Why? I can tell the guys what to do.

TOSH: No. Wahine boss no good, make da boys feel funny. Mo' betta you start raising kids—how long Mama waiting for grandchildren.

LAURA: I don't like kids. I hate kids. What you think me anyway? I get sick and tired of hearing you folks talk about . . .

(LAURA *turns abruptly and exits into the house.*)

TOSH: (*To* FUMIKO.) Why she get mad for? And she like kids, I know dat. No make sense.

FUMIKO: Well, I tink you hurt her feelings about wahine boss.

TOSH: I only told da truth.

TOKU: Laura neva mean wat she said.

TOSH: She was acting funny at home?

(AKI *comes out to the porch.*)

AKI: Aeh, wat going on? How come Laura crying?

TOKU: Well, she neva like tell you folks, but about two months ago, da doctor said she cannot have babies.

TOMI: Kawaisō.

FUMIKO: Why she neva tell me?

TOKU: I tink she was shame.

SUSAN: (*To* NOBU.) I think I'll go in and stay with Laura.

(*She exits.*)

TOSH: Mama, go talk wit' Laura, try make her feel betta.

FUMIKO: Wat I going say?

TOSH: I dunno, all da kine stuff you wahines talk. Wat your muddah said to you.

FUMIKO: We neva talk about da kine stuff.

AKI: Oi, Bāsan, you go, too.

TOMI: No call me your old woman.

AKI: Nemmine. Hurry up, all da wahines go in da house, leave da men outside by demself.

TOMI: I going, but only because I no like stay out here wit' one kūkae head like you. Sometimes you get me so mad, you ack jus' like your faddah, so bossy.

Mānoa Valley

(FUMIKO *and* TOMI *exit.* DEBBIE *stays outside, but inconspicuously.* SPENCER *looks for an opening.*)

SPENCER: Wat about USC? I can go? Get lotta 'Iolani grads on da mainland studying, and—

TOSH: No.

SPENCER: Why? You always tell me to be smart. How I going learn if I gotta stay in Hawai'i. I no like be stuck here da rest of my life.

TOSH: Mainland no good for you.

SPENCER: Wat you mean?

TOSH: Too big, you going be lost up dere. You tink so easy, but you only going suffa.

SPENCER: I know dat. But 's good for me. I like struggle by myself. I going make mistakes, but I not scared. Jus' give me da chance, 's all I ask. Da chance to go out and make it on my own. I know I can do it.

TOSH: No. Betta you stay in Hawai'i. I no like hear anymo'. Nuff already.

(SPENCER *dejectedly exits upstage left.*)

NOBU: Aeh, Spenca, wait.

(NOBU *exits. Offstage left, the dog barks.*)

TOKU: Dis time I going catch dat Elvis.

(*He exits.* DEBBIE *comes down to* TOSH.)

DEBBIE: Daddy, I know you no like me take ova your company, so I jus' made up my mind wat I going be.

TOSH: Wat?

DEBBIE: Da first woman governor of Hawai'i.

AKI: Ooohhh, 's big talk from one little girl.

DEBBIE: 'S one promise.

(*She spits in her left palm and slaps it with her right.*)

TOSH: One Kamiya promise, eh. Okay, I believe you.

DEBBIE: And I not getting married, either.

TOSH: Huh?

DEBBIE: So I can keep da family name. Debaney Masako Kamiya, governor of Hawai'i, da fiftieth state in da United States of America.

AKI: Ooohh, you so strong, you make me scared.

DEBBIE: 'S da Kamiya blood, Uncle. Strong like-a hell.

AKI: 'S right. Good for you. Go for broke, eh.

FUMIKO: (*From inside.*) Debbie!

DEBBIE: I know! Peel da daikon!

(*She runs into the house.*)

AKI: Da kids nowdays not scared of nuttin'. Run for Congress, run for governa. I neva tink nuttin' like dat wen I was young. All I know den was running for da shithouse.

TOSH: I neva figga Spenca like go to da mainland. (*Pause.*) If only Laura was one boy. She no can take ova da company.

AKI: Why?

TOSH: Well, if I stay around, okay. But aftawards, going be too tough for her. And Toku, he always going be in one corna fooling around wit' da easy stuff, and wen someting big come up, he going get his pole and go fishing by Koko Head. So wat I going do about Laura? And if I let Spenca go to da mainland, I dunno wat going happen. Da way he talk, he no like come back to Hawaiʻi.

AKI: I rememba Mama used to tell how, in da old days Japan, dey had dis funny kine style—da yōshi. If one family had a daughta and no sons, dey wen' arrange for one guy to marry da daughta . . .

TOSH: And make da guy change his name to da family's, and den let him run da family business.

AKI: Aeh, maybe Laura can divorce Toku, and you can yōshi some odda guy.

TOSH: You serious?

AKI: Nah, nah, nah. I jus' kidding. If we try da yōshi in Hawaiʻi, people going tink we crazy.

TOSH: Yeah, Japan style no good for us in Hawaiʻi.

AKI: We too American in our own funny kine way. (*Pause.*) You know, wen I wen' move to Honolulu, I felt bad about leaving you and da folks in Kona, but you can only pick so many coffee berries.

TOSH: Yeah, 's wat all us Kona kids used to tink.

AKI: Wen I told da old man I was leaving for Honolulu, how much dat wen' hurt him?

TOSH: He neva say nuttin' to me. I dunno wat he told Mama. You know da old man, you look at his face, you neva know wat he was tinking.

AKI: 'Cause he wasn't tinking about anyting. He had lotta space in his head. Sometimes I could hear da wind blowing inside.

TOSH: I know he neva like give up da farm. He really liked Kona. He used to say reminded him of Kumamoto.

AKI: But he only had lease land.

TOSH: Dat neva matta to him. Land is land so long as you can hold 'um in your hands, feel da soil. Da land was sorta sacred to him.

AKI: I guess I coulda bought da coffee land for him if I wen' stay in Kona.

TOSH: Wen da coffee berries got red and ripe, damn trees was really nice, yeah.
AKI: No tell me dat. I used to hate see da berries turn color, 'cause den we hadda climb da stepladdas and pick each ripe berry one by one. Damn, was hard work. You forget dat or wat?
TOSH: Pick da berries, wash 'um, dry 'um in da sun. Wat a life we had, eh, living in da country, good fresh air, wake up, eat rice and miso soup for breakfast, work up one sweat in da orchard.
AKI: Wat you trying to do, make me homesick for Kona?
TOSH: You know wat I like do? Go back to da old coffee land and ask da people living dere if we can pick some coffee for old times.
AKI: Aeh, I olda dan you, but I tink you came senile befo' me. Da firs' ting you do wen you try climb da stepladda again is fall off and broke your head. You clumsy, you know dat. Even wen you was one kid, like da time you wen' fall and broke your arm. Because you wen' get hurt, Mama slap me on da head. Wat Fumiko going do to me if I tell her you wen' die wit' coffee berries in your hand?
TOSH: Yeah, da old man was really scared dat time, too. He pack me in his arms and started running to Hōlualoa to see Docta Hayashi. Lucky ting Watanabe's donkey was along da road. Da old man jump on da jackass and we wen' bounce all da way to da docta. Watta sight.
AKI: Yeah, da old man was good for some laughs.
TOSH: But later wen I told him I wanted to go to Honolulu like you. Well, dat was it. Wat he going do?
AKI: No can do nuttin'. Da old man wasn't strong. He hadda come to Honolulu too, so we could take care of him. I give you credit, you wen' stay long time wit' him and Mama in Kona. Long time. You was one good son. Betta dan me.
TOSH: No, not me. Wen I found my own place, I asked da old man if he like move in wit' me; he said no, he going stay wit' you.
AKI: Not because he wanted to. Only because I was da oldest son and he tought dat was da right ting to do. Japan style.
TOSH: Wen da folks came from Japan?
AKI: Hmmm, da old man came firs', around 1896, I guess.
TOSH: Ova sixty years ago, yeah. I can still see dem busting deir ass for us, hoe hana, hoe hana every day.
AKI: Yeah, da olda I get, da mo' I tink about da old man.
TOSH: 'S funny, 'cause da olda you get, da mo' you look like da old man.
AKI: Aeh, watch wat you say, eh. Da old man was pretty ugly.

TOSH: 'S wat I mean.
(*They laugh good-naturedly. There is a pause.*)
You know wat? I neva told da old man t'anks before he died. I wish I wen' say t'ank you. You know? Jus' t'ank you.

AKI: If you wen' tell him dat, he knock your head off.

TOSH: And Mama. She work so hard wen she was young dat wen she got old, she was kinda hunched ova.

AKI: But Mama was strong. Even wen tings used to get bad in Kona, she neva cry, she neva complain. Yeah, all da Kamiya wahines tough inside. Jus' like Fumiko.

TOSH: Well, Tomi too.

AKI: Tomi? I tell you, she get one mean mout'. But inside she soft. Wen Nobu told us he going find his own place wit' Susan, Tomi ack like she no care. But dat night she wen' cry in da bedroom. But she neva let Nobu know how she feel. Me, I no care. He get his own life. But I going tell him one ting. If I die befo' Tomi, he betta take care of his muddah in his own house. As for me, all he gotta do is bring plumerias to da cemetery and clean da birdshit from my tombstone.

(SPENCER *and* NOBU *return.* SPENCER *resumes scraping the grill.* NOBU *enters the house. For a long time there is only the scraping sound on the grill.* TOSH *and* AKI *exchange glances.*)

TOSH: Spenca. I gotta talk to Mama yet. She worry about you. Not going be easy for her if you go to da mainland. Mama depend on you. I know she always ask you to do tings, but 's because she like you learn to take care of yourself. Not jus' study and play. (*Pause.*) But if you like go to da mainland, I no stop you.

SPENCER: You mean I can go? For real?

TOSH: Jus' study hard and no fool around, or I come up dere and kick your ass back to Hawai'i.

(SPENCER *runs and leaps in the air, yelling with joy.*)

SPENCER: No sweat, I going get straight A's. You and Mama no need worry. I going make good. Wait, I gotta tell Mama. Mama! Mama!
(*He dashes into the house.*)

TOSH: Aeh, Aki, we still get time today go to da cemetery and bring flowas for da old lady and old man.

AKI: 'S a good idea.

TOSH: Mama! Mama! (*To* AKI.) I going bring orchids for da old lady.

AKI: Yeah, yeah, was her favorite flowa.

(FUMIKO *comes out.*)

TOSH: Mama, we going to da cemetery.
FUMIKO: Wen?
TOSH: Now.
FUMIKO: Wat for?
TOSH: We celebrating statehood, right? Well, we going celebrate wit' our muddah and faddah too. 'S only right. Get da kids, we all go.
AKI: Yeah, tell Nobu, Susan, and Tomi. And no forget Daniel.
TOSH: Tell Debbie come out help me.
FUMIKO: (*Inside.*) Debbie!
AKI: Befo' we go, I betta take a leak.
(AKI *enters the house;* DEBBIE *comes out.*)
TOSH: Debbie, go cut some orchids so we can take 'um to da cemetery for Babasan and Jiichan.
DEBBIE: Okay.
(DEBBIE *runs off right.* LAURA *emerges and heads right, too.*)
TOSH: Laura.
LAURA: Toku caught Elvis.
TOSH: Laura, wait.
LAURA: I gotta get da leash.
(*She exits.* FUMIKO *comes out.*)
FUMIKO: Why you get dis kine last-minute idea for?
TOSH: I dunno, but I get one mo' idea. Call your sista in Hilo and talk to your muddah. Wish her happy statehood. Tell her t'anks for all da hard work.
FUMIKO: Wat hard work?
TOSH: For raising one nice daughta like you for me.
FUMIKO: You tell her yourself. Bumbai she tink I crazy.
(DEBBIE *returns with a beautiful array of orchids.*)
DEBBIE: Dis enough?
TOSH: Yeah, nice. Go tell Uncle help you cut some bird of paradise in front of da house. We go take some of dat too.
(DEBBIE *races into the house.* LAURA *enters with the leash.*)
Laura, da office really busy. I need your help.
LAURA: I busy too.
TOSH: I no mean jus' office help. I need someone to learn da business in case I get sick or someting.
LAURA: No need feel sorry for me.
TOSH: I no feel sorry for you. I feel sorry for myself, because I neva tink of you befo'. I know Spenca neva like da business, but I was going make

him take ova someting he hate—only because I was tinking Japan style. But dis not Japan. Tings gotta change. Since you da oldest daughta and not da oldest son, I wen' take you for granted. But I need you.

FUMIKO: Listen to Daddy, Laura. He no talk like dis every time, you know dat. Must be he going through change of life. Say okay.

LAURA: I gotta tie up Elvis.

TOSH: Nemmine, we taking Elvis wit' us to da cemetery. Da whole family going. Laura, Monday morning come work seven o'clock. We gotta be at da office firs' befo' da workers. 'S my numba one rule. You can learn da oddas later.

(LAURA *exits left.*)

You tink she going come?

FUMIKO: Of course. You can depend on her. How come you wen' change your mind? I neva even have to talk to you.

TOSH: I can tink for myself too, you know.

(DEBBIE *comes out.*)

DEBBIE: Okay, everybody ready.

TOSH: Good, we go.

DEBBIE: Everyting okay?

TOSH: Yeah, why?

DEBBIE: Even if Spenca go to da mainland?

TOSH: No trouble. Why, you like go mainland, too?

DEBBIE: No, I like living in Hawai'i. Hawai'i da best.

(FUMIKO *smiles and leads* DEBBIE *into the house.* FUMIKO *stops and looks back at* TOSH *from the service porch.* TOSH *is looking out over the audience where* SPENCER's *house was going to be built. There is a moment's pause, then* FUMIKO *exits.* TOSH *is alone with his thoughts, and it is very quiet. Then he turns and exits briskly into the house.*) (*Slow fade to black.*)

THE END

THE LIFE OF THE LAND

THE LIFE OF THE LAND

Time: Summer of 1980.

Place: A secluded beach park on Oʻahu.

Scenery: High bushes are upstage. Entrances are stage left, upstage from behind the bushes, and stage right. A picnic table and two benches are situated center stage. A low, manmade stone wall downstage runs across the stage. Assorted plants flourish in the area.

CHARACTERS

SPENCER KAMIYA, *forty-year-old aerospace engineer*
LAURA TANIGUCHI, *his married sister, age forty-five*
TOKU TANIGUCHI, *her husband, forty-seven*
DEBBIE, SPENCER'S *sister, thirty-four*
FUMIKO KAMIYA, *the matriarch, seventy*
AKI KAMIYA, SPENCER'S *uncle, seventy-five*
NOBU KAMIYA, AKI'S *son, forty-seven*
SUSAN KAMIYA, NOBU'S *white wife, forty-five*
DANIEL KAMIYA, NOBU'S *son, twenty*
MAXWELL LAM, SPENCER'S *high-school friend*

ACT ONE
Scene 1

(*A beautiful day, nearing noon.* LAURA *and* DEBBIE *enter from left.* LAURA *is wearing walking shorts and shirt, with slippers.* DEBBIE *has on a two-piece bathing suit with a terry cloth* hapi *coat. They clean the table and prepare it with a tablecloth. There are already picnic items on the stage: ice chest, bucket, aluminum tub, lauhala basket, etc.*)

LAURA: Not even lunch time and already I tired.
DEBBIE: Well, whose idea was get up five in da morning?
LAURA: We gotta make da lunch, eh. Anyway, you da one wanted to have da picnic.
DEBBIE: Well, since Spenca came home to visit, I tought maybe we can come out here again—like in da old days.
LAURA: Forget da old days. You too young to talk about da old days. Wait till you come old like Uncle Aki.
DEBBIE: Aeh, Uncle Aki not old. He get mo' energy dan me.
LAURA: Of all da time for Spenca to come home.
DEBBIE: Why? He had to, for Daddy's seven-year memorial service.
   (TOKU *enters from right, carrying a bucket. He wears swim shorts.*)
TOKU: Laura, Debbie, try look dis.
DEBBIE: Wat you get?
TOKU: One real surprise.
LAURA: Oh, octopus.
DEBBIE: Aaarrgghh, da real uji.
LAURA: Kinda small, eh.
DEBBIE: You wen' catch 'um?
TOKU: Of course.
DEBBIE: Still alive?
TOKU: Yeah, try touch 'um.
   (*He grabs her wrist and brings her hand toward the bucket.*)
DEBBIE: Aaaaahhhh, nnnnnoooo! Toku, noooo! Laura!
   (TOKU *breaks up, laughing, and stops.*)
LAURA: Warui no you. No tease her like dat.
DEBBIE: Toku, you almost give me one heart attack.
TOKU: Wassamadda, Debbie, you like octopus.

DEBBIE: Yeah, but I like 'um dead, not alive. Go boil 'um and make some miso sauce, den okay.
TOKU: No matta how old I get, I neva going undastand you wahines. (*He exits left.*)
LAURA: He still one kid, no. Sometimes I wonda why I wen' marry him.
DEBBIE: Because of da kid in him.
LAURA: Den I wonda why you wen' divorce Elton.
DEBBIE: Because of da kid in him.
(*They laugh and resume preparations for lunch.*)
LAURA: Debbie.
DEBBIE: Yeah?
LAURA: Mama not going be happy if you run off wit' Jeremy.
DEBBIE: I know. She making me crazy. She still think I going back to Elton. I told her, "No way, Mama, Elton is da past. Jeremy is da future." But you know Mama, she still old-fashioned. She doesn't believe in divorce.
LAURA: Where Spenca?
DEBBIE: I dunno. Max and him probably roaming around some place. Why? Someting wrong?
LAURA: No.
DEBBIE: I notice you acting kinda funny toward Spenca.
LAURA: Can tell?
DEBBIE: Sure. I not blind.
LAURA: I jus' no like he stay around now.
DEBBIE: Why, wat he did?
LAURA: He always had bad timing.
DEBBIE: It's about da business, yeah?
LAURA: Why people no can keep da area clean. (*She picks up some rubbish and throws it in a large trash can.*) No consideration for odda people.
DEBBIE: Laura, you heard me?
LAURA: Afta Spenca go back to L.A., den you can write him da news if you like.
DEBBIE: Me? I don't care if he knows, but you acting like—
LAURA: I just no need Spenca here now. For wat he came back anyway; he no care about da family. All he care about is himself. He was always da spoiled one. Get everyting his way.
DEBBIE: Well, maybe if you talk to him, he might undastand . . .
LAURA: Look, one penny. Maybe my luck going change.
(*She picks it up. There is laughter upstage behind the bushes.*)

DEBBIE: I going get my camera.
(*She exits left.*)
LAURA: Wait, no go now.
(SPENCER *and* MAX *enter.*)
SPENCER: I really love dis place.
MAX: Not bad.
SPENCER: Haven't been here since I was one kid.
MAX: 'S nuttin'. I live in Hawai'i all my life and I neva been here before.
SPENCER: My faddah used to bring us here wen we were young. 'S right, eh, Laura?
LAURA: Yeah.
SPENCER: Still some places on O'ahu where you can get away, eh.
MAX: If I like get away, I go on a junket to Vegas.
SPENCER: I bet Hawai'i people travel more dan anybody else in da world.
MAX: Yeah. Every time you look up, somebody you know flying off to somewhere. My Auntie Jane jus' got back from Canada. One nodda uncle and auntie going off to Europe. My bruddah and his wife wen' to da Orient last year. It's a wonda dey no all get lost.
SPENCER: Good old island fever. 'S one reason why I left Hawai'i.
(LAURA *exits left. The men go to the stone wall.*)
MAX: See da sights around da world and leave Waikīkī to da tourists.
SPENCER: It's too bad, all da giant condos on O'ahu. Too much, eh. Huge phallic symbols rising in da sky—erect, demanding—a massive jungle of concrete pricks looking for a climax.
MAX: Chee, you get vivid imagination, yeah. You on drugs or someting?
SPENCER: Hawai'i has sure changed from da fifties wen we were in high school.
MAX: True. But you changed, too. You not da same person who left Hawai'i twenty-one years ago. Wen you wen' up, you was good-looking. Now you look at you. (*Shudders.*) No wonda you not married yet.
SPENCER: Aeh, not my fault. I asked dis girl in L.A. to marry me. But she said no. Hell, we even lived together for six months.
MAX: Yeah, 's one good ting about living on da mainland. You can shack up wit' one wahine and nobody bodda you. If I did dat here and my muddah find out—good night—she probably chase da girl out wit' one broom, den wack me ova da head.
SPENCER: To her you still one sixteen-year-old virgin.
MAX: Aeh, she my muddah, eh, why break her heart. She deserve one pure son—if only in her mind.

SPENCER: Get married and make your muddah happy.

MAX: No mo' time. Gotta keep moving, gotta stay young. Aeh, I saw Nakasone last month at da bank. Da bugga was dragging his ass, man. 'S wat four kids do to you.

SPENCER: Well, I was ready to settle down. But Gwen said no. You believe dat?

MAX: Sure. You ain't no prize.

SPENCER: Aeh, listen. I said, "What's wrong? You found somebody else?" And she said, "All you men think that. You always think there's someone else. I just don't want anyone tied to me. I don't need it."

MAX: Hoo, da tough wahine. Make my you-know-wat shrivel up.

SPENCER: So I said, "Then why are we living together?" And she said, "Because it's convenient." Can you beat dat? Convenient. Like I was da corner drugstore or someting. I was a convenience.

MAX: Yeah, we live in da age of convenience. We have pouch-bag dinnas, douche-bag cleanas. We aerosol our armpits and pollute da atmosphere da same time. I can undastand why some people wanna go back to nature. Keep tings simple. Make life easy.

SPENCER: But some people don't like it dat way. Dey want to make things complicated. Dey like complex relationships.

MAX: I know, I know. Like women, right? Dey make too many demands. Dey expect too much. I told dis wahine, "No make fuss, no make me nervous, no mess up my life." But she no give up.

SPENCER: Who dis wahine?

MAX: My muddah.

SPENCER: Max, I'm trying to be serious.

MAX: Aeh, my muddah is da mos' serious woman I know.

SPENCER: Well, anyway, Gwen and I broke up.

MAX: Where she was from?

SPENCER: Texas.

MAX: Oh, no wonda. 'S wat you get fool around wit' one Texas girl. You tink one Hawai'i girl going tell you dat. Hawai'i girls da bes', no forget dat. I gotta introduce you to some nice local girls. But before I do dat, how 'bout we hit da bars tomorrow night?

SPENCER: Cannot. Got a memorial service for my faddah. Make it da next night.

MAX: You got it. Aeh, rememba wen you came home afta graduating from USC and I took you to all da bars around town?

SPENCER: Yeah, dis one bar maid at Nihonbashi really liked me. She was kinda pretty.

MAX: Aeh, dose bar girls look good in da candlelight glow, but take 'um out in da bright light of day, and dey make your liver cringe.

SPENCER: No get jealous. Just because she liked me betta.

MAX: Aeh, once I met dis bar girl who really looked terrific in da booth. Dim light, you know, cozy atmosphere. And she was getting me hot, rubbing my thigh wit' her hand. Chee, I tought I was falling in love. I told her, "Aeh, darling, you like go see one samurai movie at Toyo Theata?" So we wen' set one date for one matinee. Wen I saw her in da daylight, I almost faint. She look like Boris Karloff.

SPENCER: She wasn't dat ugly.

MAX: Look like his twin sista. Maybe I was half drunk in da bar, I dunno, but afta dat I neva trust da lighting in bars.

(DEBBIE *returns with a camera and a bag of camera supplies.*)

DEBBIE: No tell me you guys still talking about da old days.

SPENCER: Not just da old days, Debbie. Da good old days.

DEBBIE: Wat you trying to do, recapture your youth?

SPENCER: Nothing can replace da fabulous fifties. . . . Where you going?

DEBBIE: I wanna see wat kine shots I can get dis side.

(*She exits right.*)

MAX: Aeh, Spense, wen you going back to L.A.?

SPENCER: I dunno. Maybe neva.

MAX: Wat?

SPENCER: I got nobody waiting for me dere. Not now, at least.

MAX: I tell you one ting. Lotta guys came home from da mainland. Dey neva like it up dere.

SPENCER: L.A. not bad, especially Redondo Beach, where I live. Betta dan most places. But, I dunno, maybe because I turned forty. But I wonda if I neva make one mistake moving to da mainland.

MAX: But you hadda live up dere because of your job, right?

SPENCER: Yeah, 's where da job was. But now I kinda get dat feeling, you know, but I still neva make up my mind yet. Maybe, just maybe, time to come home.

MAX: Hawai'i calls to her native sons to return to her shores. (*He uses his hands to make a horn-like sound, like blowing into a conch shell.*)

AKI: (*Offstage.*) No, no, no, how many times I gotta tell you.

SPENCER: No say nuttin' yet.

MAX: Yeah, no worry.

(AKI *and* DANIEL *enter from upstage.*)

AKI: You listen to me, I no steer you wrong. 'S wat grandfaddahs fo'—to give advice. And I tell you wat grandsons fo'—to listen to dat advice.

DANIEL: But why can't I be a nurseryman like you?

AKI: No talk dumb like dat. Aeh, Spenca, talk to your cousin Daniel.

SPENCER: What's up?

DANIEL: Well, all I'm saying—

AKI: He like take ova da nursery afta I retire. (*To* DANIEL.) You like your muddah get mad at me or wat? She neva send you to University of Hawai'i so you can be one nurseryman.

DANIEL: It was partly your fault. I always helped you in the nursery during the summers. I learned everything from you.

AKI: Dat was my mistake. (*To* SPENCER *and* MAX.) You see dis kid? He smart and he stupid. Nobu and Susan send him to Punahou School so he can go Harvard or Yale and become one docta or lawya. No, he like go UH. Okay, go. Den he like study philosophy. Fo' wat? No need go school fo' dat. Wen I was young, da bes' philosophers I heard neva had education. But dey was dere in 'A'ala Park sitting on da benches talking about life. Make sense too, wat dey said. It says right dere in da book: "A nurseryman cannot be a philosopher and a philosopher cannot be a nurseryman."

DANIEL: What book?

AKI: Da Grandpa Aki Book of Life.

SPENCER: Uncle, I don't see why Daniel can't be a nurseryman.

AKI: Spenca, you live on da mainland too long; you no count. Max, wat you tink? You going buy one hibiscus plant from him if you know he was one philosopher?

MAX: Chee, Aki, I hate hibiscus.

AKI: (*To* DANIEL.) You see.

DANIEL: That's not an answer.

AKI: 'S good enough for me. I gotta go, get someting to do.

(AKI *exits right.*)

SPENCER: Old age hasn't changed Uncle Aki one bit.

DANIEL: He knows what the nursery means to me. I like working the soil with my hands; it feels good. During the summers, I lived at the old house in Kalihi with Grandpa.

(AKI *returns.*)

AKI: Aeh, where da toilet around here? I tought was dat way.
MAX: You like go benjo? C'mon, I show you. I gotta go too.
AKI: I not going embarrass you if I have to stop behind one bush, eh?
MAX: Me okay, I dunno wat da bush going say.
(*They exit upstage behind the bushes.*)
SPENCER: Funny. My father wanted me to take over his building contractor company, but I had other ideas. I wanted to be an aerospace engineer.
DANIEL: That's the point. You did what you wanted to do and you're happy. I should be able to do what I want too.
SPENCER: Yeah, it's important. Sorta sounds like the way I felt years ago when I told my father I wanted to go to the mainland. Good thing Laura was able to help my father and take over the company after he passed away.
DANIEL: Uncle took your decision okay?
SPENCER: Huh?
DANIEL: Uncle Tosh. He wasn't mad or anything like that?
SPENCER: My father? Oh, no. I don't think so. Well, we never really talked about it.
DANIEL: What projects have you worked on? Viking? Venus? Things like that?
SPENCER: No, mostly military stuff. Can't really say much because of security reasons.
DANIEL: Sounds exciting.
SPENCER: Danny, your career—you sure about yourself? Maybe you should think it over some more. You don't want to disappoint your parents.
DANIEL: Well, it's a tough decision, but I know what I want.
TOKU: (*Offstage.*) Watch out, now.
FUMIKO: (*Offstage.*) Okay, okay.
(TOKU *helps* FUMIKO *by holding one arm.* LAURA *carries a half-filled bag of seaweed.*)
TOKU: Aeh, Spenca, we pick some seaweed for you.
SPENCER: Yeah? Chee, only half a bag? When we were kids, we used to bring home at least two bags.
LAURA: Mo' and mo' people learning da taste of ogo.
(FUMIKO *sits on the bench.* TOKU *exits left.*)
FUMIKO: Even da mempachi hard to find. Not like befo'.
LAURA: Yeah, we gotta search da markets for da fish. Ohtani's at 'A'ala Park or Tamashiro's in Kalihi.

SPENCER: I don't even see memachi in L.A. fish markets. Aeh, let's look tomorrow.
LAURA: Toku can take you.
SPENCER: Toku never change, eh.
LAURA: Toku? Wat you mean?
SPENCER: You know, he still take it easy, eh. Daddy used to kid about Toku running off to go fishing all the time.
FUMIKO: Toku no go fishing like befo'. He really work hard. He was one good son-in-law to Daddy. He listen to Daddy, help him. I neva hear him talk back to Daddy one time.
LAURA: 'S right.
(TOKU *returns, stops at a distance.*)
TOKU: Aeh, Mama, you see da blanket ova dere, by da tree?
FUMIKO: Yeah.
TOKU: I wen' lay 'um out for you unda da shade. Go 'head, go rest.
FUMIKO: Oh, good, but I not tired now.
TOKU: You sure? You know wat, I go lie down dere little while, test 'um out for you.
(AKI *and* MAX *enter from upstage.*)
FUMIKO: Oh, okay.
(TOKU *exits.*)
AKI: Wen we going eat?
LAURA: Still little early, Uncle. Anyway, we gotta wait for Nobu and Susan.
AKI: No make Max wait too long, eh. His stomach was growling like one gorilla in one cave.
MAX: Aeh, bull lie, no believe him.
LAURA: Okay, Uncle, we go to da car. I get oranges you can snack on.
AKI: Only orange?
LAURA: I no like spoil your appetite.
AKI: (*To* MAX.) You like orange?
MAX: I eat anything.
AKI: Okay, Laura, go get da oranges for us.
LAURA: You not coming wit' me?
AKI: No ask one old man like me walk too much. I going stay here talk story wit' Max.
LAURA: Danny, can you help me?
DANIEL: Sure.
(*They exit left.*)

AKI: How come your muddah wen' name you Maxwell?
MAX: She love Maxwell House Coffee.
AKI: Lucky ting she neva like Chock Full O' Nuts.
  (*They proceed downstage to the stone wall out of earshot of* SPENCER *and* FUMIKO.)
FUMIKO: Where Debbie?
SPENCER: She went to take some pictures.
FUMIKO: Dat girl, no can stay still even fo' one minute.
SPENCER: Why she wen' divorce Elton?
FUMIKO: No can do nuttin'. Daddy wen' try so hard for dem. He even put dem in da back house he was planning for you. Dey neva have to pay rent. Daddy wanted Elton at least get his degree from UH. Now we dunno where Elton stay.
SPENCER: Daddy was planning da back house for me?
FUMIKO: Huh?
SPENCER: Da back house. Was for me?
FUMIKO: Dat was his idea, but dat was befo' you wen' to da mainland.
SPENCER: Mama, I neva know dat.
FUMIKO: Oh, he wen' build da house anyway to rent out. Lucky, though, 'cause Debbie living dere now.
SPENCER: How come you and Daddy neva tell me about da house?
FUMIKO: Wat Daddy going say? No go to da mainland and I build you one house in da back? He had in his head you going get married, raise kids, so da back house was perfect. Especially if you was going work wit' him in da business and take ova for him someday. But not important now. Where Debbie? Go look for her.
SPENCER: Mama, wen I left for da mainland, Daddy was mad at me?
FUMIKO: Fo' wat you ask da kine question now? Baka, no. Dat was long time ago.
  (DANIEL *enters from left with beach-type chair, zabuton, and plastic bag with oranges. He gives the oranges to* AKI.)
DANIEL: Auntie, come sit in this chair, more comfortable.
FUMIKO: Oh, t'ank you, Daniel.
  (TOKU *enters with a fishing pole.*)
TOKU: Mama, I going fish little while. Tell Laura call me wen lunch ready.
FUMIKO: Okay, go, go.
MAX: Get good fishing around here?
TOKU: Depends, yeah. We go.
  (*They exit right.* DANIEL *exits left.*)

AKI: Spenca, wen you going back mainland?
SPENCER: Oh, I was thinking I might stay till Mama go on her Japan trip.
AKI: Your Buddhist group travel like-a hell, eh?
FUMIKO: Wat else us widows going do? All da husbands die, so we gotta go in bunches.
SPENCER: I guess Daddy was too busy to travel.
AKI: Well, da business meant everyting to him.
FUMIKO: He tought if he leave da business for one minute, someting bad was going happen.
AKI: He neva care travel, anyway. Once in a while, he like go back see Kona, but 's all.
FUMIKO: You, too, Aki, you jus' da same. You neva go any place.
AKI: Aeh, da Las Vegas trip was enough. (*To* SPENCER.) Couple years ago I wen' on dis five-day gambling junket. I sign dis paper, dey give me chips. I shoot craps, sign one mo' paper, get mo' chips. By da time I was ready to go home, I lost two tousand dollars. Make me sick. Wen I was young, took me one year to earn dat much. Wen I get old, I lose all dat in five days. 'S da trouble nowdays—inflation.
(DEBBIE *and* LAURA *enter from left.*)
FUMIKO: Debbie, I was worried about you.
DEBBIE: Oh, Mama, you always say dat.
SPENCER: You took your pictures already. Fast, eh?
DEBBIE: Sure, I'm not middle age like you.
AKI: 'S right, no. You old man already.
SPENCER: Yeah, Uncle, forty years old.
AKI: Good night! Dat means me wat? Sixty-eight, eh?
LAURA: No, no, you no can cheat like dat. You going be seventy-six dis year.
AKI: Bull lie! How can? Only yestaday I wen' get married, my boy Nobu was born, I build up my nursery. Only yestaday, I tell you.
DEBBIE: Uncle, you still young—young enough to get married again and start one whole new family.
AKI: I not dat young.
DEBBIE: Too bad, I was going find one wife for you.
AKI: Nemmine me. You get your bruddah here not married yet.
DEBBIE: Oh, no worry about him. He going find one mainland girl. 'S right, eh, Spenca.
SPENCER: Yeah, lotta girls up dere.
DEBBIE: 'S Toku fishing?

SPENCER: Yeah.

DEBBIE: Toku, wat you catch?

(*She exits.*)

LAURA: Mama, Debbie made up her mind. She going to da Middle East wit' Jeremy.

SPENCER: Middle East? What for?

LAURA: Some photojournal assignment.

SPENCER: Not dangerous?

LAURA: She doesn't think so.

FUMIKO: You da olda sista; tell her no go.

LAURA: Good chance for Debbie. If she no go now, she going always feel bad.

FUMIKO: I know, but, she cannot run around da world jus' like nuttin'. Wat if she get hurt?

LAURA: You cannot hold her back. She's not a baby. 'S her life. You let Spenca go to da mainland and he was only one kid.

SPENCER: Yeah, but that was different.

LAURA: Wat different? Because you were a boy?

SPENCER: No, not that, but—

LAURA: Den why Daddy neva let me go to a mainland school wen I wanted to go?

SPENCER: You never wanted to go to the mainland.

LAURA: How you know? You could read my mind? All you thought about dose days was yourself. Anyway, dis isn't your problem.

SPENCER: How long would Debbie be gone?

LAURA: Two months.

SPENCER: Why so long?

LAURA: Jeremy wants to take Debbie to England on da way back, show her where he grew up. Look, Spenca, I did wit'out your questions all dese years, I can do wit'out dem now.

AKI: Aeh, you folks, about time you came.

NOBU: (*Offstage.*) Hello, everybody!

AKI: Hungry, you know. Everybody waiting to eat.

(NOBU *and* SUSAN *enter from left.* NOBU *carries a picnic basket.*)

SUSAN: I know. Late again. Sorry. Hello, Fumiko, how are you?

FUMIKO: Oh, good. Everyting okay.

SUSAN: That's good. I brought some food, Laura.

LAURA: You didn't have to.

SUSAN: I felt like playing housewife.

NOBU: Aeh, who's that stranger over there?

SPENCER: Hi, Nobu.
NOBU: Susan, look at this old man. Auntie, we better get Spenca married before too late.
FUMIKO: Yeah, go find one wife for him.
SUSAN: Spencer, it's so nice to see you again.
SPENCER: Susan, you're looking great.
AKI: How come you took so long?
NOBU: Sorry, Pop, I was talking to a few of my future constituents.
SUSAN: He's determined to get elected this time.
NOBU: I feel so confident, it's frightening. My time has come.
SUSAN: He was proposing an offshore gambling casino, three miles off Waikīkī.
NOBU: You know how much money Hawai'i people gamble away in Vegas?
SPENCER: Tons of it.
NOBU: Right. My way, we keep most of that money in the state, where it can do some good. Hell, even Pop dumped a bundle in Vegas.
AKI: You too late. I already confess.
NOBU: All that gambling money, we can use for welfare, education, senior citizen programs.
(MAX *enters from right.*)
SPENCER: Oh, Susan, Nobu, I want you to meet my buddy from high school days—Max Lam.
MAX: Hi.
SUSAN: Nice to meet you, Max.
NOBU: Max Lam? Nobu Kamiya. Where do you live?
MAX: Where do I live? Ah, in a two-bedroom condo. But, ah, I use one bedroom as an office.
SUSAN: He wants to know if you're in his voting district.
MAX: Oh, Pearl City.
NOBU: There goes another vote. Never mind, we still gotta talk. Got some ideas I want to throw at you. No curves, straight down the middle.
AKI: Well, let's eat, kau kau time.
NOBU: You come from a big family?
MAX: Four sisters and one brother.
NOBU: Lots of aunts, uncles, cousins?
MAX: Too many.
NOBU: Good, good.
(NOBU *and* MAX *exit left.*)
LAURA: Toku, Debbie, kau kau.
SUSAN: Brought your favorite, Aki. Nishime.

AKI: No kidding. (*He opens a container.*) Spenca, you believe one haole can make good nishime?

SUSAN: It's not that good.

AKI: Try taste.

SPENCER: Hmm, 'ōno.

AKI: Told you. Susan smart cook Japanee food.

(DEBBIE *enters. She hugs* SUSAN *from the back.* SUSAN *reacts affectionately.*)

FUMIKO: Not enough room here.

LAURA: I guess we can go on da grass unda da tree.

FUMIKO: Aki, we go move ova dere.

AKI: Wat, I jus' started to eat dis musubi.

LAURA: Gomen, gomen.

FUMIKO: You lucky your daughta-in-law kawaigaru you.

SUSAN: Oh, he's my pet.

AKI: No can help, I'm so cute, yeah.

SUSAN: Now, Aki, don't get a swell head.

LAURA: Okay, everybody, we moving ova dere.

(*The women gather up the items to exit left.* DANIEL *enters from upstage.*)

DANIEL: Hi, Mom.

SUSAN: Hello, dear.

(*She pecks him on the cheek.*)

AKI: You know, Susan, you da bes' daughta-in-law I eva had.

SUSAN: I'm the only daughter-in-law you ever had.

AKI: No, is dat right? How you like dat.

(*They exit left.* TOKU *enters.*)

SPENCER: Catch anything?

TOKU: No mo' luck.

(*He exits left.* SPENCER *sits alone at the picnic table. There is general chatter and laughter offstage.*)

LAURA: (*Offstage.*) Spenca, you like one engraved invitation or wat?

(SPENCER *looks offstage, then slowly walks off as the lights fade to black.*)

Scene 2

(*A half hour later.* LAURA *and* TOKU *enter.*)

TOKU: Why you drag me away from da food? I neva finish.

LAURA: We had enough.

TOKU: No, no. Jus' because you full, dat no mean I full.
LAURA: I wanted to tell you someting.
TOKU: Why you neva tell me ova dere?
LAURA: I no like Spenca hear.
TOKU: Why, you going talk stink about him?
LAURA: Not dat. Now listen. I no like you mention da business and wat I going do. I no like Spenca know.
TOKU: He going find out soona or later.
LAURA: Yes, but not now.
TOKU: You shame of someting?
LAURA: Shame of wat?
TOKU: About me. I know I wasn't dat much help wit' da business.
LAURA: Not dat.
TOKU: I know Spenca going tink I neva do enough.
LAURA: You did plenty.
TOKU: But no can help, eh. I no mo' da kine head.
LAURA: Toku, Toku, listen to me. Wat you trying to take da blame for? Not your fault. I jus' no like give Spenca da satisfaction of—
(SPENCER *and* MAX *enter.*)
MAX: Boy, I sure wen' eat.
LAURA: Promise, no say nuttin'.
TOKU: Okay, I try, but . . .
MAX: I think I betta go on a diet. Look at dis.
(*He sticks out his stomach in an exaggerated manner.*)
SPENCER: You in really sad shape, man.
MAX: Aeh, wait. Not dat bad, eh? (*He now sucks in his stomach and struts around lightly.*) How's dis? Love me, love my incredible body.
SPENCER: Aeh, Toku, you finish eat already? We left plenty behind.
TOKU: No, I gotta eat some mo'.
LAURA: Have to clean up.
TOKU: Wait, wait, no clean up till I finish eating.
(*He scoots off as* LAURA *follows.*)
MAX: Dat Toku is one nice guy.
SPENCER: Yeah.
MAX: Good, eh, stay wit' your family like dis. Betta dan live alone on da mainland.
SPENCER: Maybe. You notice my sista Laura act sorta annoyed at me?
MAX: No. But, you know, some sistas li'dat. Dey get in deir moods, auwe, look out, bruddah, head for da hills.
SPENCER: Well, I'm getting some strange vibrations from her.

MAX: My sista Sherry, wen she get cranky, she spit fire at everybody. I dunno how she do dat. She shoulda been one magician.

(SUSAN *and* AKI *enter.*)

SUSAN: I think Danny will do well at Yale.

AKI: Oh yeah, dat kid smart. No need worry.

SUSAN: Be honest with me, Aki. Am I interfering in his life?

AKI: You his muddah, he going listen to you. Or I kick his ass.

SUSAN: I just want him to be happy, and in the long run I know he won't regret it.

AKI: You right, you right. He belong in Yale.

SPENCER: Danny's going to Yale?

SUSAN: We hope so. I want him to study on the mainland, like you, Spencer.

SPENCER: Ha, I'm not a good example.

SUSAN: But it was worth it. Look at you. Successful, educated—

MAX: Crazy.

SPENCER: He's right. Yeah, when I was young, I couldn't wait to get to the mainland. I had enough of Hawai'i at the time. So I traveled to new places, saw new faces. What about you, Susan? Been back to Michigan often?

SUSAN: No, after my mother died, there wasn't much point. Hawai'i is my home now. As a child, I grew up on an island, then I move thousands of miles away to live on another island.

MAX: No kidding. You lived on an island—in Michigan?

SUSAN: Yes, a place called Grosse Ile.

MAX: Gross Eel? Why, they have lots of fat moray eels there?

SUSAN: Eels? Oh no. Grosse Ile is French for Grand Island. G-R-O-S-S-E I-L-E.

SPENCER: (*Laughing.*) 'S wat you get live in Hawai'i all your life. Moray eel, cheez.

MAX: Aeh, watch dis moray eel bite you.

(*He grabs* SPENCER's *arm and pretends to gnaw on it.*)

SPENCER: Aeh, aeh, watch it, look out!

(*They fall to the ground, tangled up.* NOBU *and* DANIEL *enter, talking to each other.* NOBU *dumps rubbish in a trash can upstage left.*)

SUSAN: Are you hurt?

SPENCER: No, no, just a little friendly wrestling we used to do in school.

MAX: Yeah, in the sixth grade.

AKI: See wat happen wen you guys no get married—you neva grow up.

NOBU: Susan, can we see you a minute?
SUSAN: All right. Excuse me.
(SPENCER *gives* MAX *a friendly shove.*)
SPENCER: Make ass, eh, you.
MAX: Me make ass? You make ass.
(AKI, SPENCER, *and* MAX *sit at the picnic table.*)
NOBU: How are you feeling?
SUSAN: Fine. Why?
(NOBU *takes out his stress card from a shirt pocket.*)
NOBU: Here. Hold this card with your thumb and let me see if you're under any stress.
(*She holds the card as requested.*)
SUSAN: Oh, Nobu, I'm perfectly happy and at peace. You know I don't believe in this card anyway.
NOBU: I have something to tell you. Or Daniel does. But let me see. (*He takes the card back.*) Well, the color is blue. You are under no stress.
SUSAN: I told you.
NOBU: Okay, put your mother under stress.
DANIEL: I want to become a nurseryman.
SUSAN: A what?
DANIEL: A nurseryman, like Grandpa.
SUSAN: Did he say . . .
NOBU: Nurseryman, yes.
SUSAN: I don't believe . . . what is this, a joke? I'm not laughing. Please don't joke with me. I . . . I . . . what? What?
NOBU: (*To* DANIEL.) You see what you did. (*To* SUSAN.) I told him he was crazy. But I can't get through to him. He says his lifelong ambition is to be a nurseryman. You figure it out.
SUSAN: Danny, you're not serious.
DANIEL: Yes, I am. I've thought it out seriously and carefully.
SUSAN: Wait, your grandpa will have something to say. I was just talking with him.
(SPENCER *motions to* MAX *that they go and they exit behind the bushes. The others go to* AKI.)
AKI: I know, I know. I told him he was crazy. I no like one crazy guy work for me. Crazy guys go into politics like Nobu.
NOBU: That's right. They don't call me Crazy Kamiya for nothing.
SUSAN: Honey, with your education and your mind, you could be so much more. No offense, Aki.

AKI: 'S okay, you right. I became one nurseryman because I neva had education.

DANIEL: There's nothing wrong with being a nurseryman.

SUSAN: Of course not. But you could do more good being something else.

DANIEL: The nurseryman belongs to an honorable profession. You work with the land, growing plants and trees and making our environment livable. In the future, the nurseryman will become even more important when our natural resources are destroyed, when cement replaces greenery, and glass and steel cover Hawai'i. Nurserymen will keep the Islands green, fighting against a hostile mentality. Where developers lay cement, nurserymen will plant life. We will be the last bastion of sanity in a world gone mad with clanging machines, ravaging technology, and devastating sterility.

SUSAN: How long did you rehearse that speech?

DANIEL: About a week.

SUSAN: Honey, you sound just like your father.

DANIEL: Is that supposed to be a compliment?

SUSAN: No.

NOBU: What?

SUSAN: I'm sorry, dear. (*To* DANIEL.) What I mean is, you and your father sometimes get caught up in your own ideas and go nowhere, like a cat chasing its tail.

NOBU: When do I do that?

DANIEL: Mom, the work begins with the land. It's what the Hawai'i state motto says: "Ua-mau-ke-ea-o-ka-'āina-i-ka-pono"—The life of the land is perpetuated by righteousness.

NOBU: Susan, you can't fight the way he feels.

SUSAN: I want something more for him.

NOBU: It's his life.

SUSAN: You want him to be a nurseryman?

NOBU: Of course not. It's a dumb idea. But we Kamiyas are real smart in coming up with dumb ideas. It's in the Kamiya blood. I think what I'm doing is right and nobody's going to stop me. It's the same with Danny. He can take care of himself. A good fight never hurt anybody.

SUSAN: I can't fight the two of you.

DANIEL: It's not your fight, Mom.

SUSAN: Yes, it is. I didn't marry your father and raise you just so I could stand on the sideline and watch you screw up your life.

NOBU: Now cool down, honey. You have to understand that Danny is obstinate, just like my father.

AKI: Obsti wat? No use da kine hybolic word about me, eh. I dunno if you talking stink or wat.
DANIEL: It means you're stubborn as a jackass.
AKI: Okay, dat I undastand. 'S true.
NOBU: Let's take a walk. There are some people by the banyan tree I haven't met yet.
SUSAN: Campaigning again?
NOBU: Give me your thumb. Right here. Check your stress.
(*He steers her off left.*)
SUSAN: I haven't finished with Danny.
NOBU: Later. The fish will still be in the pond when you return with fresh bait. Red. Bright red. High-level stress. STRESS in capital letters.
(*They exit.*)
DANIEL: I didn't think Mom would be the hard case.
AKI: Well, dat shows you dunno your muddah dat good.
DANIEL: She's so busy with her society junk, running around—benefits, parties, meetings.
AKI: She gotta do lotta dat to help your faddah.
DANIEL: He still hasn't been elected.
AKI: Your muddah put all her strength in you from wen you was one baby.
DANIEL: Yes, how do I love thee, son, let me count the ways.
AKI: Aeh, aeh, aeh, watch your mouth. I get ova fifty years more hard living dan you, so I figga I know wat I talking about. You listen to me. Your muddah eva tell you about her bruddah Roy?
DANIEL: Only that he died in the war.
AKI: Iwo Jima, 's where he wen' ma-ke. And your grandfaddah in Michigan, Mason, well, Roy was his only son. And wen your muddah told her family she like marry Nobu, dat was like one bomb wen' explode. Her faddah was mad like-a hell. He said if she marry one Jap, she no need come home, eva. Was only twelve years afta da war, you undastand, so was tough on your muddah. But she had guts. Your muddah get mo' guts dan you, me, and your faddah put togedda. So she got married anyway and came to Hawai'i to live. And in dose days, your muddah had to face my wife, Tomi, your grandmuddah. You rememba her as one fussy old lady. Well, I tell you, she was one fussy middle-age lady wen your muddah came. Was not so easy deal wit' your grandmuddah. So your muddah had to struggle here too, but she made it.
DANIEL: Yeah, I see that part, but—
AKI: Aeh, no but me. I no like but. Okay, now I going talk to your Japanese side. Your Michigan grandfaddah wen' die long time ago before he

saw you. So I know your muddah like show him: "See, Papa, see your grandson, Daniel Mason Akira Kamiya, is a . . . professor of philosophy at Yale . . . is da president of da United States." But wat she can say now: "Look, Papa, my son da nurseryman."

DANIEL: Yes, I want my life to mean something, but I wanna do it my way.

AKI: Your way, my way, dis way, dat way. Listen now, I going tell you one las' time. No tink I going back you up on dis. I not going let you disappoint your muddah da way I wen' disappoint my muddah long time ago. See, my muddah wanted me to stay in Kona help wit' da farm. But I said no, I ain't no stupid coffee farma. And I wen' run away to Honolulu. And wat I did dere? Gamble, fool around, waste my time. I neva forget da stupid tings I did to my muddah and my faddah. You neva forget da hurt inside.

DANIEL: But you know how good I am in the nursery. You need me. I won't disappoint you.

AKI: I no need you. No tink I need you. Nemmine me. Your muddah mean a lot to me. And you mean a lot to your muddah. Make your muddah happy, and you make me happy. Sometimes you gotta do wat you no like do. Sometimes you gotta make da sacrifice.

(FUMIKO, LAURA, *and* DEBBIE *enter from left;* SPENCER, *from right.*)

AKI: Aeh, Fumi, you came jus' in time. You like go bat'room?

FUMIKO: No, not yet.

AKI: C'mon, c'mon, we go. I lonesome go myself.

FUMIKO: Okay, okay.

AKI: Good, we can talk story and go. Danny, you come, too. I like tell you about my muddah, your great-grandmuddah. She was really good at cleaning ears wit' one hairpin, especially my ears.

(AKI, FUMIKO, *and* DANIEL *exit upstage behind the bushes.*)

SPENCER: Mama sure got old.

DEBBIE: Wat you expect, Super Mom or something?

SPENCER: No, but the way she walk.

LAURA: Da arthritis no help.

SPENCER: When did she get arthritis?

DEBBIE: Long time already.

LAURA: Sometimes at night I gotta rub da Ben-Gay on for her. You know, Spenca, you missed out on lotta family things since you been on da mainland. Wat are memories to us mean nothing to you.

SPENCER: I guess so.

DEBBIE: Like da time Daddy fell off da stepladda and konk his head.

SPENCER: Wat?

LAURA: Wen Uncle Aki found out wat happened, he told us to neva let Daddy climb one stepladder, 'cause he always falling off, even wen he was a kid.

DEBBIE: Yeah, but Daddy only had a concussion. But I neva know dat. I hadda drive him to da hospital 'cause nobody else was home. I was so scared.

SPENCER: Why?

DEBBIE: Why? Hooo, Spenca, 'cause 's da first time I saw Daddy get hurt. You neva saw him helpless. right? He was always helping us. He was always da strong one. So wen I saw Daddy lying on da ground, I screamed so loud all da birds in da mango tree flew out like crazy.

SPENCER: Then what happened?

DEBBIE: I said, "Daddy, Daddy, you okay?" And he gave me dis funny kine look, so I tought I betta drive him to da hospital jus' in case. And I got him in da car and I was driving, and I forgot where Kapiʻolani Hospital was.

LAURA: Yeah, and you go past dere almost every day.

DEBBIE: I know, but I was unda pressure, right. You can't blame me. So I said, "Daddy, where da hospital went?" And he said, "Put da pig in da ground." Man, den I really got scared. So I hadda stop at one service station for help. Da guy tried to give me directions, but I was fading out, so he jumped in and drove Daddy and me to da hospital.

LAURA: Tell him who da driva was.

DEBBIE: Oh yeah, was Elton, my husband.

LAURA: Your ex-husband.

DEBBIE: Yeah, yeah, yeah, my ex-husband, my ex-husband.

(TOKU *shuffles in from left, wearing swim shorts and looking like he just came out of the ocean.*)

TOKU: Debbie, you no going swim?

DEBBIE: No, I no like wet my hair. I get one date wit' Jeremy tonight.

(TOKU *lies down and puts his head on* LAURA's *lap.*)

LAURA: Get up, your hair all wet.

TOKU: No can help, da ocean not dry.

(*She pushes him up.*)

Max still swimming.

DEBBIE: Spenca, one thing you missed wen you were on da mainland was Toku's cooking.

SPENCER: Yeah?

TOKU: Well, Laura was too busy to cook so I hadda learn.
SPENCER: What's your best dish?
DEBBIE: Chicken heka.
TOKU: Yeah, I guess so, chicken heka. I wen' learn from your muddah. Except I put in one special ingredient—Chivas Regal.
SPENCER: Expensive chicken heka, eh.
TOKU: I tell you, if you put in da right amount at da right time, taste tarrific. Even da president of da United States can eat my chicken heka.
SPENCER: Chee, too bad you can't open a restaurant, eh.
TOKU: Aeh, you know, 's wat I was tinking too. I told Laura afta she sell da business, we should start one restaurant.
SPENCER: Sell what business?
TOKU: Sorry, wen' slip outta my mouth.
LAURA: I selling da business.
SPENCER: Daddy's contractor business?
LAURA: Yeah.
SPENCER: Yeah, what? You gotta tell me more than that.
LAURA: 'S da bes' ting we can do.
SPENCER: Why? I don't undastand.
LAURA: You don't have to undastand. Not your problem.
SPENCER: I don't think you should sell.
LAURA: You have nuttin' to say about it.
SPENCER: Why not? My name's Kamiya too.
DEBBIE: Too late, Spenca.
SPENCER: How Mama feel?
TOKU: No worry about your muddah, Spenca. We going always take care of her.
SPENCER: I'm not talking about that.
TOKU: I know how you feel, but—
SPENCER: No, you don't know how I feel.
LAURA: No blame Toku.
SPENCER: I'm not blaming him, but I got something to say about all this. You're not gonna sell the business so easy. Daddy worked so hard on it. Man, I don't like what I see.
LAURA: Wat do you see? Tell me, maybe we all blind but you.
SPENCER: Okay, so you and Toku got tired of the business, and—
LAURA: We didn't get tired of da—

SPENCER: And maybe you think you're gonna make a lotta money selling it, but you know how much it meant to Daddy. And no tell me Mama doesn't care 'cause I know better. When you took over the business, it was your responsibility to keep it going.

LAURA: Responsibility? Look who talking. Wat about you? Twenty-one years ago you went to da mainland knowing Daddy wanted you to continue da business afta he retired.

SPENCER: Yeah, and you didn't like the idea. You wanted it for yourself.

LAURA: No be stupid!

SPENCER: Look, you have the business. I don't care. But don't throw away everything now just because you wanna do something else.

TOKU: Spenca, was not so easy as you tink. No get mad witout hearing da odda side.

LAURA: Toku wen' work all dese years in da business, a job he hated. He didn't have to. Wasn't his faddah's business. But he worked hard for Daddy. Not like you.

TOKU: Laura, c'mon already, nemmine da kine stuff.

LAURA: (*To* SPENCER.) Sure, was nice for you. Go off to SC and work on da mainland, do wat you like, nobody to worry about but yourself. You tink you had it tough up dere, studying and working?

SPENCER: Yeah, was hard, but I did it.

LAURA: Yeah, go 'head, pat yourself on da back. Big deal! 'S nuttin' compared to da work we had to do. Wat did you achieve on da mainland? Wat did you do dat was so great or important? Tell me dat, tell me wat da—

TOKU: Laura, 's enough! No talk already.

(TOKU *exits left.*)

LAURA: Don't you eva look down on Toku or me. Don't you eva! (*She strides off. There is an awkward pause.*)

DEBBIE: You were wrong, Spenca.

SPENCER: What, you turning against me too? Before, it was always you and me against Laura.

DEBBIE: Dat was wen we were kids. Things change. Laura's been real good to me. She backed me up lots of times. Wen I had trouble wit' Elton; wen I wanted to study photography; wen I started to date Jeremy and Mama was against it. I think Laura was right in a way. Wen you went to da mainland, you cut off a part of da family—like losing an arm or a leg. But da wound you left is healed now. We got used to not having you around.

SPENCER: What about Mama? How does she feel about giving up the business?

DEBBIE: Oh, Spenca, wat if you neva went to da mainland, wat if you stayed and helped Daddy. Wen you were on da mainland, did you eva think of those things? Were you too happy to think of us? Could you have made things betta if you had stayed home?

SPENCER: I dunno. I guess my mind was on other things. But I thought everything was fine at home.

DEBBIE: I missed you, Spenca, I missed not having my bruddah around. Laura not going admit it, but I know even she missed you, in her own way. And Mama and Daddy. I think dey missed you most of all.

SPENCER: I gotta talk to Mama.

DEBBIE: No bodda her now. Let her rest today. She get enough headache wit' selling . . . da Kamiya Corporation, and wit' me.

(*She exits.* SPENCER *stands alone, lost in thought as lights dim to black.*)

ACT TWO
Scene 1

(*Later in the afternoon.* DANIEL *enters with steel wool and an implement to clean the barbecue grill. He works methodically.* TOKU *enters.*)

TOKU: Cleaning da grill already?

DANIEL: Yeah.

TOKU: You like I do 'um for you?

DANIEL: No, that's okay.

TOKU: Me good for da kine work, you know, no problem.

DANIEL: Thanks, but I better do it.

TOKU: Going get 'ōno barbecue tonight.

DANIEL: I hope you made the special Toku Taniguchi barbecue sauce.

TOKU: Oh yeah. Big demand all da time.

DANIEL: You really like cooking, yeah.

TOKU: Well, guy like me, neva wen' past high school, so I cannot do da kine heavy head work. Make da head sore. So I wen' find someting simple—cooking. I watch, ask questions. Like, wat rosemary and nutmeg good for, why you put da bay leaf in da stew? Den I try mix certain stuff togedda to make da kau kau taste mo' 'ōno. Sometimes hoooo da big mistake, but sometimes broke da mout', man.

DANIEL: Trial and error. That's how scientists work too. Great.

TOKU: Yeah? Not bad, eh. But 's nuttin'. See, like you—you always make da honor roll. And you was valediction of your class, eh. Too good, man. If I get your kine head, I make good use. Instead of cooking, I try do someting good for da world. Make da world undastand dat people gotta live togedda and no fight. But you gotta be smart and get good education, so you no shame talk to anybody. You lucky your parents smart, so you smart too. Get connection, you know. See, my faddah dumb like one termite, so wat me? Son of da termite. No mo' head, only good eat wood.

DANIEL: Nah, Toku, you've always been a terrific guy.

TOKU: Oh yeah. I'm a tarrific guy, I know dat. But I'm a dumb tarrific guy. Aeh, by da way, I always brag about you to my friend. See, he was always telling me how smart his nephew. Like wat da hell I care. So I tell him my nephew one hundred times smarta dan his nephew. By da way, I hope okay if I call you my nephew, even though you not really my nephew. We no mo' even da same blood.

DANIEL: No, I like it. My Uncle Toku.

TOKU: 'S good. At leas' I can say I get one smart nephew who going to Yale and who so smart he going make da Kamiya family bust all buttons on da shirt because dey so proud. I tink everybody get deir dreams on you. Me too. Danny, someday you going make all our dreams come true.

DANIEL: But what about you, Toku? You have your own dreams.

TOKU: Nah. My kine dream nuttin'. Catch da biggest fish in da world. Da biggest crab or lobsta. Small stuff li'dat. Nuttin' serious. Nuttin' to change da world.

DANIEL: I thought you said once you wanted to be a professional fisherman.

TOKU: Oh, dat. Nah . . . well. If I had da money, long time ago, maybe, yeah. Get one fleet of fishing boats, go out and catch all da fish we can. You know, hook 'um, heave 'um back, hook 'um, heave 'um back, one afta anodda. Woulda been good fun. Yup. But dat was long, long time ago.

DANIEL: You don't feel bad about that? Your dream and . . .

TOKU: No, no. Dat was da dream I had befo' I got married. My biggest dream was hoping Laura and me can have our own kids, maybe raise one boy like you, so I can teach him how to fish. But Laura neva can have babies, so . . .

DANIEL: You and Laura could've adopted.

TOKU: 'S wat I told Laura. But, you know, she was so busy helping her faddah wit' da company. No mo' time to raise one baby, eh. And afta she became da boss, mo' worse. Da company was her baby. She sacrifice everyting for da company.

DANIEL: You too.

TOKU: Nah. My life too small to sacrifice. But you, you diff'rent. You can make great tings happen, we all know dat.

DANIEL: That's a heavy load to carry. Maybe too heavy.

TOKU: Yeah, I can see all of us hanging on your back. Get room for everybody or wat? Aeh, but no need worry, 'cause you one Kamiya. If you was one Taniguchi, den I pity you, and I jump off your back befo' you fall down. But you going do good, 'cause you cannot let down your Grandpa. He like brag all ova da place about you. He always saying he only had t'ird-grade education, but his son is one lawya now, and his grandson going be even betta. Here, lemme do dat. 'S one job for me. Go, go. Go read one book or someting. Or go someplace and tink about someting. Use your head, no let 'um get lazy. Aeh, wait till you taste my Korean barbecue.

(*He takes over for* DANIEL, *who exits.* TOKU *scraps the grill, happily singing as he works. The song is an old, popular Japanese ditty, "Tsuki ga Detta, Detta."* NOBU *enters.*)

NOBU: How you doing, Toku?

TOKU: Good, good. You?

NOBU: I don't know. Mixed emotions. You always seem to have a good sense of who you are.

TOKU: Yeah, I guess so. Not so hard. My name is Toku Taniguchi, I was born Kaka'ako side in da year—

NOBU: That's not really what I meant.

TOKU: Oh . . . den I cannot help you.

NOBU: I know. I have to work it out myself.

TOKU: Nobu, I can ask you someting?

NOBU: Sure, be my guest.

TOKU: You no get tired talk to people you dunno?

NOBU: No. Because everybody's different, that's the point. Rich or poor, educated, uneducated, young or old, no matter. They have their own stories to tell. So I try to get to know them better, to make the extra effort, so I can serve them well.
TOKU: Sound like hard work.
NOBU: Yes, it is. But you know, if I can't meet new people and talk to them, I'd probably shrivel up and die.
TOKU: If you was me, you woulda died long time ago.
NOBU: Toku, you know Kennedy was forty-one when he was president. I'm already forty-six.
TOKU: Well—
NOBU: A young-looking forty-six, I know. But still four years away from the mid-century mark. Can you believe it? Where the hell did time go?
TOKU: I dunno. You wen' look every place or wat?
NOBU: Oh, I looked high and low, from one end to the other. Time just passed me by and didn't even say hello.
TOKU: Yeah, yeah. We about da same age. How I look?
NOBU: You look good too. Use Pond's cold cream at night before you go to bed. Helps keep the skin moist. (*He takes out the stress card.*) Ah, let me test you. Here, put your thumb over this spot.
TOKU: Wat dis for?
NOBU: Testing your stress factor. I'm curious. Stress is a killer. We want to keep our stress level low; we don't want heart attacks or strokes. Okay, let me see. Yeah, I thought so.
TOKU: Wat?
NOBU: Your color is blue. Deep blue.
TOKU: Someting wrong wit' me?
NOBU: No. It means you're absolutely calm and relaxed. You can't get any calmer than that. That's good
TOKU: Wat about you?
NOBU: That's what I'm checking. Outwardly I may seem calm but . . . hmmm, red. Flaming, hellish red.
TOKU: 'S good?
NOBU: Bad, real bad.
   (*He stands and tightly clenches his fists, arms bent at the elbows. Eyes are shut. His body is tense for ten seconds. Then he completely relaxes and sits, head down, arms dangling at his sides.*)
TOKU: You okay?

NOBU: Yeah, just a relaxation exercise.
TOKU: Chee, I tought you was having one heart attack.
(DEBBIE and SUSAN enter from right and stop.)
DEBBIE: I wanna tell you something, but don't tell anyone, not even Nobu. Promise?
SUSAN: Of course. Bad news?
DEBBIE: I got a job offer to be a staff photographer for the Star-Bulletin.
SUSAN: Deb, that's wonderful.
DEBBIE: But I turned it down.
SUSAN: Why?
DEBBIE: It's a job I dreamed about for so long, and now . . .
SUSAN: It's Jeremy, yeah?
DEBBIE: He wants to return to England—to live. Can you see me living in London?
SUSAN: Well, at least they speak English there. If you lived in Japan, you'd be helpless. I probably know more Japanese than you now.
DEBBIE: Why do you think I never dated Japan guys. That would be something, marrying some guy from Japan and moving to the old motherland. I'd be a screwed-up foreigner in the land of cherry blossoms.
(DANIEL enters.)
DANIEL: Hi, I was thinking what kind of clothes I would need in Connecticut. Any ideas?
SUSAN: What?
DANIEL: It snows a lot, right?
SUSAN: You mean you're going?
DANIEL: What is it, six thousand miles away?
SUSAN: What happened?
DANIEL: I guess I'm just a son of Eli and didn't know it. (He kisses her on the cheek and exits.)
SUSAN: Nobu, Nobu, did you hear?
NOBU: What?
SUSAN: Danny. He said he's going to Yale.
NOBU: How'd you persuade him?
SUSAN: I didn't say a word, not a word.
NOBU: You see, I told you. The power of silent persuasion.
SUSAN: You don't sound happy.
NOBU: Of course I am. But I also know that Danny's just starting out, and I'm not going to get too excited or worried at this point in his life. I don't need the stress.

SUSAN: Oh, you and your stress. I'm just so happy for Danny.
(LAURA *enters*.)
SUSAN: Laura, Danny's going to Yale, after all.
LAURA: That's great. What'd you say to him?
SUSAN: Nothing. I said nothing.
LAURA: Well, it worked.
DEBBIE: Let's go tell Uncle Aki.
SUSAN: Yes. Where is he?
LAURA: That way.
(SUSAN *and* DEBBIE *exit left*.)
LAURA: Uncle and Mama washing up.
NOBU: They took a nap?
LAURA: Yeah. Funny, no, wen you get old, you move so much slowa. But time is running out on you, so you should be moving fasta to do all da tings you wanna do. Mother Nature is all screwed up.
NOBU: You're right. And Time is my enemy.
TOKU: Nobu, befo' I used to go crabbing in Kaneohe Marine Base. Sometimes I caught Samoan crabs dis big (*He indicates the size of a catcher's mitt*.) But da military says da area is a bird sanctuary now and we hadda get out. No fair, eh. We no hurt da birds, so why we cannot catch some crabs. Da crabs must be monstas by now.
NOBU: Sounds like the military is being arbitrary about this. I'll contact the provost marshal and see what I can do. For good public relations with the local people, the military should reconsider its positions. I'll start the ball rolling on Monday.
TOKU: Chee, t'anks, eh.
NOBU: My pleasure. . . . Who's that with Max?
LAURA: Don't know.
TOKU: Neva saw dem before.
NOBU: Me too. Think I'll go say hello.
LAURA: Good luck.
NOBU: Thanks.
(*As he exits, he takes out a small bottle of breath freshener and sprays into his mouth*.)
TOKU: You know wat I was tinking? Afta your muddah come back from Japan and rest up, why da t'ree of us no go visit California.
LAURA: Wat for?
TOKU: We can see San Francisco, visit Spenca in L.A., den go Vegas for few days.

LAURA: Nah. Take Uncle Aki wit' you to Vegas. 'S enough.
TOKU: Wat about you? No mo' fun if you no go.
LAURA: I no feel like going.
TOKU: Good for you, get away little while.
   (AKI *and* FUMIKO *enter.*)
LAURA: About time, you folks. Susan found you?
AKI: Yeah, yeah.
LAURA: Well, we go take a walk dis way, exercise little bit.
AKI: You and Toku go. Me and your muddah go stay here talk story.
TOKU: C'mon, Aki, we walk slow.
AKI: No, no, you go. We going get mo' fun sit here talk about da old days.
LAURA: Okay.
   (LAURA *and* TOKU *exit right.*)
AKI: Good, yeah, take a nap little while.
FUMIKO: Yeah. Bad habit.
AKI: Getting old.
FUMIKO: Yeah, makule. Wen I was young, I used to climb da mango trees, and my muddah used to say, "Abunai, bumbai you pilikia!" And I always yell back, "Not dangerous for me. I was born in da year of da monkey!"
AKI: Sometimes I wish da kids could see me wen I was young and sassy. I was one sportscar den. Woooosssshhhh! Now dey look at me, and dey see one Model-T jalopy. (*He pretends he's steering a bouncy jalopy.*) Chukka lakka chukka lakka chukka lakka. Aeh, how you like da ride, Fumi?
FUMIKO: Jus' like we riding down one old Kona road.
AKI: Yup, 's da way used to be. You miss dose times?
FUMIKO: Well, we used to work hard, but if I look back now, I tink we had a good life. You too?
AKI: Hmmm. We always had food to eat, clothes to wear. Living in Kona was special, I guess. Good weather, lots of fruits to eat, plenty fishing. Da simple life.
FUMIKO: But dose days, I neva tink I going be old like dis. Wen my muddah was getting old, I used to tink, why she gotta walk li'dat, why she forget tings, why she always complaining dis part hurt, dat part hurt. And she tell me, "Someday you going find out wat I mean." Sure enough, now my body doing da same ting to me.
AKI: Same wit' me. Now my koshi sore. (*Indicates his lower back.*)
FUMIKO: Me here now. (*Rubs her shoulder.*)

AKI: Sometimes here sore. (*Touches his ankle.*)

FUMIKO: Mine worse. Right here. (*She stands and bends over and rubs both calves.*)

AKI: How 'bout dis? Hiza-bonsan. (*Rubs kneecaps.*)

FUMIKO: But my hands too.

AKI: Wait, you no can say dis. My oshiri sore, da bone. (*Rubs his rear end by the tail bone.*)

FUMIKO: Oh . . . my oshiri okay.

AKI: Yeah, da jalopy getting ready for da junk yard.

FUMIKO: Well, you still da bes' jalopy I know.

AKI: T'anks, eh. You always had smart mout'. (*Looking out over the ocean.*) Hmmm, I feel like I standing out by Keauhou Bay now. 1923. I wen' out dere one las' time befo' I wen' leave Kona for Honolulu.

FUMIKO: How old you was?

AKI: Nineteen. . . . Nine-teen. I used to hate pick da coffee berries dose days. Hard, hard work. Sometimes I get so mad, I used to sneak off go fishing. Wen I come home, my faddah used to yell at me. But he always eat da fish I wen' catch. It's a wonda he neva choke on da bones. I always gave him da stink eye.

FUMIKO: I know. You was really one rascal dose days. Tosh used to tell me.

AKI: Yeah, I was bad. But funny how I turn out so good, eh.

FUMIKO: Miracle.

(SPENCER *and* DANIEL *enter.*)

AKI: I gotta admit, sometimes I miss da old Kona. Nowdays, you see all da hotels along da Kailua-Kona coast. Not da same. But nice fo' da tourists.

SPENCER: Had a good rest, Mama?

FUMIKO: Oh yeah, 's one ting, I no mo' trouble sleeping.

AKI: You lucky. Me, sometimes I no can sleep, so I go out in da nursery and walk around da plants or sit unda da *plumeria* tree.

DANIEL: Once, I came in the morning and found him asleep under the tree. I thought he was dead.

AKI: 'S not one bad way to go. Unda da clear Hawaiian night sky, wit' all da stars twinkling, you jus' slip away.

(NOBU *and* MAX *enter.*)

NOBU: With the Hawai'i Land Trust Act, you actually get an alternative way of owning real estate.

MAX: Yeah, I read about that in da *Advertiser*, but I didn't pay much attention.

NOBU: See, under this law, the trustee, say a bank, holds the legal, equitable title of the property. But you as the buyer would keep what we call "beneficial interest," which means you can occupy, manage, finance, and even sell the property.

MAX: If I ask you to repeat what you just said, you think I might understand what you just said?

AKI: Max, go buy someting on da Big Island in Kona, den I can come visit you.

NOBU: Talk about Kona. There's the Paradise Garden Villas in Keauhou-Kona. A furnished, two-bedroom, two-bath unit on fee simple land, you can buy for two hundred eighty thousand.

AKI: Two hundred eighty thousand! Fumi, I neva tought Kona land going be wort' so much.

FUMIKO: Yeah, our days was only country wit' lotta *kiawe* trees.

AKI: We had dis one house. My faddah and one neighbor, Yamada-san, wen' build 'um. Only trouble, my old man neva know nuttin' about being one carpenta. And Yamada-san was real cockeyed. No kidding. So da work was real kapulu. Da house was so lopsided, I used to fall down all da time and roll around on da floor.

(DEBBIE *and* SUSAN *enter.*)

SUSAN: Can you believe those women? Somebody should say something to them.

DEBBIE: Well, they gotta be tourists.

SUSAN: Even so. They should know better than to go around naked.

NOBU: Women naked—on the beach?

SUSAN: Yes, two haoles.

NOBU: Are they attractive?

SUSAN: What difference does that make?

NOBU: Well, nothing. Those women probably don't know the law. I'd better investigate this.

MAX: I'll go too, in case they only speak Chinese and you need a translator.

NOBU: Thanks, Max.

(*They exit.*)

AKI: Susan, you sure dey naked?

SUSAN: Very naked.

AKI: Oooohhh. Well, I gotta go use da bat'room.

(*He proceeds upstage, then slowly turns to go stage right.*)

SUSAN: Aki!

DEBBIE: Uncle, shame on you.

AKI: Aeh, wassamadda. I'm old, but I not dead.
(*He exits.* SUSAN *and* DANIEL *remain upstage, while the others stay downstage.*)
SUSAN: Grandpa is so funny.
DANIEL: Yeah, he's amazing. I don't think he'll ever retire. He'll never give up his nursery.
SUSAN: Someday he'll have to.
DANIEL: I don't want Grandpa wasting away in an old folks' home.
SUSAN: We wouldn't let it happen. He'll stay with us. Don't underestimate your father. He knows the right thing to do. And he loves Grandpa more than he shows. You should see that.
DANIEL: If anything happens to Grandpa and he needs me, I'll come home and never leave.
SUSAN: Yes. I understand.
SPENCER: Mama, why you like sell da business?
FUMIKO: I no like sell.
SPENCER: But Laura said she selling—
FUMIKO: No can help. Wat I can do?
SPENCER: No let her. 'S your business. Daddy left 'um for you.
FUMIKO: But Laura do all da work. She da boss.
SPENCER: Tell her how much da business mean to you.
FUMIKO: She wen' try her bes'.
SPENCER: Why she wanna quit for?
FUMIKO: You talk to her.
SPENCER: I tried, but you know Laura.
FUMIKO: Too late, anyway.
SPENCER: No say dat.
DEBBIE: Spenca, you only making tings worse.
FUMIKO: All wat Daddy work for gone. From one small company he struggle and build 'um up, but now. . . . Daddy was so happy wen da company reach da twentieth anniversary. He wen' make one big party. 'S wen you was on da mainland and neva like come home. At da party, Daddy said, "Good, eh, Mama, everybody enjoying demselves. In twenty mo' years we go make one mo' party like dis." No can make da party now.
SPENCER: Mama, no listen to Laura.
DEBBIE: Not dat easy. You dunno wat happen. Da business climate wen' change. Some construction firms couldn't make it. High interest rates, soft economy, less construction. Was really bad.

SPENCER: Dammit, Laura should've handled the business betta.
DEBBIE: Not her fault.
SPENCER: Sure it is. Gotta be.
(NOBU and AKI enter.)
NOBU: Susan, you have to be more precise when you describe a situation to a third party.
SUSAN: What's wrong?
NOBU: Those women were not naked.
SUSAN: They were too.
NOBU: They were topless. There is a distinct and visible difference between naked and topless.
SUSAN: So you were disappointed.
AKI: No, he was okay. I was disappointed.
SUSAN: Oh, Aki, you were not.
(LAURA and TOKU enter.)
LAURA: Guess wat? Max talking to da naked girls.
NOBU: They were topless, not naked. Right, Toku?
TOKU: No ask me. Laura wen' cova my eyes.
NOBU: Well, the girls are from Lyon, France. When they go to the Riviera, they go topless, so they didn't think—
SUSAN: How do you know they're French?
NOBU: How do I. . .
AKI: No look at me. You da lawya. I like see you talk your way outta dis.
DEBBIE: Don't be too hard on Nobu. After all, he is the father of your son.
NOBU: Yeah, where would Danny be without me?
AKI: And where would you be wit'out me? And where would I be wit'out my faddah? And where would my faddah be—
DEBBIE: Uncle, we get da message.
AKI: Yeah, no get me started about da generations. Jus' give us second generation some credit—da nisei.
SUSAN: I think you nisei are wonderful.
AKI: I tink so. Yeah, we hadda deal wit' da old Japan style of our parents and learn da American way too. Was not so easy. 'S like trying to eat one whole T-bone steak wit' only chopsticks. But we tried our bes'.
DEBBIE: Right!
(She hugs AKI.)
AKI: Someday da nisei going all pass away and going be up to you, da sansei, to carry on. You gotta teach da yonsei da meaning of kurō. Susan, dat means hardship. Be like da issei, da firs' generation, my muddah and faddah. Dey had hard times, but dey was tough.

LAURA: I rememba dem as quiet and relaxed. Nuttin' seemed to bodda dem.

AKI: Me, wen I was one kid, I wen' bodda dem. I used to grumble about everyting. Monkutade, dat was me. Now I say, "Okāsan, Otōsan, I'm sorry. Gomen nasai." (*Slightly misty-eyed.*) How you like dat? I'm seventy-five years old and I still apologizing to my parents. Excuse, eh. (*He takes out a handkerchief and wipes his nose as he exits upstage, followed by* DANIEL.)

DEBBIE: You know what I was thinking, Susan? What if Danny decides he likes it in Connecticut or Rome or wherever and never returns to Hawai'i?

SUSAN: Wherever he goes, there'll always be a little bit of Hawai'i in him, and he can spread the aloha spirit around the world. He belongs to the universe.

NOBU: I married the eternal romantic.

DEBBIE: Our grandparents came from Kumamoto, Japan, to Kona, Hawai'i. Our parents left Kona for Honolulu. Spenca went from Honolulu to Los Angeles. Danny, the fourth generation, is off to Connecticut. Who knows, maybe Danny's grandchildren will want to live in a colony on Mars.

NOBU: I wonder what the real estate development will be like there.

DEBBIE: Instead of island fever, they'll have planet fever.

TOKU: Da only person neva wen' anywhere is me. I neva even left dis island.

LAURA: That's gonna change. Soon as da business is sold, we're gonna travel all ova. I don't want you to be like Daddy. He neva went any place but da Big Island and O'ahu.

DEBBIE: He was always too busy.

FUMIKO: Toku, you go. No make da same mistake like my husband.

DEBBIE: Thanks, Toku.

TOKU: Fo' wat?

DEBBIE: For being there when we needed you.

NOBU: Spenca, remember the party your father threw to celebrate statehood?

SPENCER: Sure. The summer of '59.

TOKU: Man, dat was some party. I ate so much laulau my unko was black fo' two days.

(*The women around him move away in playful disgust.*)

LAURA: Kato-san was so happy and drunk, he was dancing around like a geisha.

DEBBIE: I had my first taste of sake.

SUSAN: And I'll never forget you, Fumiko, when you ended the life of that poor chicken.

DEBBIE: Yeah, I couldn't eat chicken for a long time after that.

TOKU: Laura, we should make one party for da working boys, you know, one las' time togedda.

NOBU: Spenca, I remember you asking your father if you could go to USC to study.

SUSAN: To be an aerospace engineer. And you made it, exactly what you wanted to be.

NOBU: The passion you had then to be in aerospace. I could see it in your eyes.

SPENCER: That was a long time ago. Probably sound ridiculous now if I say I'm gonna give it up and return to Hawai'i for good.

NOBU: Yeah, that would be funny.

DEBBIE: You joking?

SPENCER: What do you think?

SUSAN: I think you're serious.

SPENCER: It would be easy to do. The physical part at least.

FUMIKO: Wat about your job in Los Angeles?

SPENCER: They can replace me in a second. I'm not that important.

SUSAN: But all those years you put in your career.

SPENCER: The career? Just a job, nine to five, and collect my paycheck.

NOBU: What about that passion you had for aerospace?

SPENCER: I lost it. Somewhere between heaven and Earth. Yeah, I had dreams of building spaceships and going to the moon. Instead, I got tied up with military projects—working on missiles that kill innocent people, women and children. And you work on these projects for years, then see them canceled. And then guys are always quitting and joining other companies, and then returning, not because it means something to them, but only because of higher salaries or promotions.

FUMIKO: No quit your job now. Wat people going say. Shame if you come back. Pohō if you waste everyting now.

SPENCER: But Mama, I can help you—

LAURA: Listen to Mama. Go back to L.A. We don't need you now.

SPENCER: I thought you would say that. You're throwing away the family business because you got tired of it, and you don't want me here to remind you.

The Life of the Land 129

(AKI *and* DANIEL *return from upstage but don't join the group. They listen from the bushes, hidden from the others.*)

LAURA: I don't care wat you think. You don't mean a damn thing to me. You think now you can come home and tell me wat I gotta do? Wat do you know about wat happened while you were having a good time on da mainland? Now I gotta listen to you, my wise little bruddah who went to da mainland? You want me to take notes while you tell me wat to do? Who da hell are you? Nobody! Nobody!

SPENCER: Aeh, is it my fault you screwed up the business?

LAURA: I did not.

SPENCER: Then who? Who's responsible?

DEBBIE: Spenca, done is done. Pau, finish.

SPENCER: Mama, don't let Laura do it.

FUMIKO: I no blame Laura. She wen' work hard for Daddy. If you feel like dat, why you neva stay in Hawai'i and help Daddy. He had big ideas. He wanted you to take ova someday, but you neva care about dat. Afta you wen' to da mainland, Daddy neva say one word against you, but I know he was hurt. Jus' like you wen' stab him in da heart.

LAURA: Mama, we go home. Toku, let's go.

(LAURA *and* TOKU *exit.*)

NOBU: Spenca, Laura just ran into bad luck. It finally came down to risking bankruptcy or selling now and making sure the workers still had jobs. That was Laura's concern. She could've been stubborn and fought to the end, but she didn't want to hurt the workers. This way, they can keep their jobs. She made sure the other company wouldn't fire her workers. It's in writing. I handled it.

DEBBIE: You know, a lot of them—like Kato-san—were with Daddy from way back. Laura was worried especially for da olda workers. It's for the best, Spenca, really. I no lie to you.

(NOBU *and* SUSAN *exit.*)

SPENCER: Mama, if I wen' stay home, you think maybe I could have saved the business?

FUMIKO: *Shiran.*

SPENCER: Don't say you don't know. Tell me.

DEBBIE: Mama, Laura was Daddy's bes' worka. Rememba, Daddy said dat one night. He said nobody worked harda dan Laura and dat da working boys all respected her. Dat made Daddy real happy. Rememba? He was so proud of her.

(FUMIKO *nods.*)

SPENCER: Mama, I wish I could make things betta. I wish I could push time back to 1959 and change everything. I would make it all the way you wanted. I'm sorry if I . . . I . . .
(AKI *and* DANIEL *enter.*)
AKI: Aeh, Spenca, today wen I look at you from da back and I saw da way you walk, I tought sure was your faddah all ova again. Yō nitoru, eh, Fumi?
FUMIKO: Yeah.
SPENCER: I wonda.
AKI: You cannot see yourself da way I see you, but 's da true fact. Yup. Blood is strong. You know, me and your faddah we used to always talk about dis and dat, and I tell you one ting. He neva had bad feeling in his body for anybody. He was like dat from kid time. Real good-hearted guy. And if you was happy on da mainland, den he was happy for you. Because he undastood wat you was feeling.
SPENCER: I hope so.
AKI: Yeah. He knew. 'Cause he was young once too. And dat time Kona was too small for him. Well, 's all I going say, 'cause I dunno wat else to say.
(LAURA *and* TOKU *return. His arms are filled with items.*)
LAURA: Mama, you ready?
AKI: Aeh, where you folks going?
LAURA: Home.
AKI: Wat you mean? Too early.
LAURA: Too late.
AKI: Toku, you said you going make Korean barbecue.
TOKU: Yeah, but Laura like go.
AKI: Nemmine Laura. Me da old fut in dis family; you listen to me. C'mon, I hungry. You was bragging about your special recipe. I like taste.
TOKU: We go stay.
LAURA: No.
(TOKU *looks at* AKI *and the others.*)
TOKU: Laura, we staying!
(*He drops everything on the ground.*)
AKI: Okay! I help you folks. Where da charcoal, where da . . . We staying! Aeh, dat was good.
(*He slaps* TOKU *on the back as they exit.*)
DEBBIE: I'll get da charcoal. Come on, Laura, come.
(*They exit.* MAX *returns.*)

MAX: Spense!
(SPENCER *goes to him, away from his mother.*) Aeh, I get two French chicks waiting for us. We go.
SPENCER: Now?
MAX: Aeh, dey not going wait till Christmas. Next week dey flying to Tahiti. I made one date for us tomorrow night.
SPENCER: I told you I get my father's memorial service.
MAX: Oh yeah. I forgot. I was so excited. (*He goes to the ice cooler and takes out three soda cans.*) Dat means I gotta handle two by myself. Might kill me. Wat da hell, I die happy.
(LAURA *and* DEBBIE, *carrying the charcoal bag, return and go to* FUMIKO.)
SPENCER: Well, I guess no harm talk to da wahines.
MAX: Right. We get some culture if nuttin' else. Mrs. Kamiya, I going borrow your son little while.
(*They exit.*)
FUMIKO: I wen' get mad at Spenca. I dunno why.
LAURA: I know how much da business meant to you, Mama. Spenca neva have to tell me dat.
FUMIKO: Da business gone. Me good for nuttin', 's why. No mo' head. I neva can help you.
LAURA: No, Mama, not dat.
FUMIKO: Wen Daddy firs' started da business, I told him, "Let me go to da office, I can do someting." But he always said, "You stay home, take care da kids." I wish I wen' force him to let me help. I wish . . . but I'm so stupid, wat I can do?
LAURA: No say dat, please. You wen' help plenty. Wit'out you, Daddy couldn't do anyting. Because you wen' work so hard at home, Daddy could concentrate on da business side.
DEBBIE: 'S right, Mama. Da work you did at home was so important. You raised us. We were so lucky.
FUMIKO: I was hoping even though Daddy wen' die, he was still going help you run da business.
DEBBIE: He did, Mama. Laura kept it going a long time.
LAURA: Maybe Spenca could've done betta.
DEBBIE: No, not Spenca. He would've been bad, because his heart wouldn't have been in it. I bet he would say da same ting. You did good, Laura; nobody could've done betta.
LAURA: Kato-san came ova to me da odda day, and he said he was sorry for wat happen. He felt like was his fault.

FUMIKO: Kato-san Maui boy. From Kahului. He play hard, but he work hard too. 'S wat Daddy liked about him.
LAURA: Afta Daddy wen' pass away, and couple guys wen' work for somebody else, Kato-san told me, "No worry, Laura, da res' of us going stick wit' you all da way. I talk to dem already." He made me cry. I going miss dem. I dunno wat I going do witout da business. Mama . . .
(LAURA *cries.* FUMIKO *tries to console her, but she weeps too.*)
DEBBIE: It's not da end of da world. It's jus' da end of . . . da Kamiya Corpora . . . 's wat I hate about being Japanese. Too damn dopey about stupid things. . . . I neva mean dat. Laura, Mama, I'm sorry. It's just I . . .
(*There is a tableau with* DEBBIE *and* LAURA *on either side of* FUMIKO, *linked by arms and hands. They sit in sorrowful silence as the lights fade to black.*)

Scene 2

(*It is after dinner.* SPENCER *and* MAX *enter.*)

MAX: I promised da girls we going take dem to see Don Ho Tuesday night. We let him do da work, get 'um in da mood. I tell you, da French wahines no going get chance. Da Don Ho show is like one aphrodisiac—da wahines go halulu. Foolproof plan.
SPENCER: Yeah, like da time we wen' double date and wen' up by Hanauma Bay to see da submarine races.
MAX: Dat was wen we were juniors in high school. Dis different. Now we go to my condo. I take Chantal to my bedroom, you take Anik to my office.
SPENCER: Chee, t'anks. Really romantic, your office.
MAX: No get picky. Use da couch in dere. Lumpy, but not bad.
SPENCER: Afta I return from L.A., I going find me one nice local girl and get married.
MAX: Yeah, forget da haole wahine from Texas.
SPENCER: Who said she was haole?
MAX: She from Texas, right?
SPENCER: So wat? Gwen's Chinese.
MAX: Oh, no wonda. Aeh, Chinese wahines tough minded; you gotta watch out. I should know.
SPENCER: Well, da main thing is dat I'm coming home. Who said dat, "You can't go home again"?

MAX: You can't go home again. . . . My muddah said dat.
SPENCER: Aeh, I'm serious.
MAX: You dunno my muddah. She said everyting once in her life. Afta I got outta da Army, I was going home to live, but my muddah said, "You cannot come home, go out and work and no loaf around."
(NOBU, SUSAN, *and* DANIEL *enter*.)
NOBU: Spenca, you definite about returning home?
SPENCER: Yeah, made up my mind. Twenty-one years on the mainland is enough. I wanna walk around in my bare feet again.
SUSAN: What would you do here?
SPENCER: Oh, I got some money saved up. Some stocks. Made some good investments. I'll sell my condo in Redondo Beach. I didn't blow it all away in a wild and crazy life. Maybe I'll buy a saimin stand.
(DEBBIE *returns*.)
NOBU: Let me know if I can help you in any way.
SPENCER: Thanks, Nobu. I appreciate it.
SUSAN: We'll see you at the memorial service.
SPENCER: Yes.
SUSAN: I'm glad you're coming home.
SPENCER: Thank you.
NOBU: See you, Max; you got my card.
MAX: Yeah, t'anks. (*To* DANIEL.) You need help? Here, let me.
(MAX *helps carry some items. All exit except for* SPENCER *and* DEBBIE.)
DEBBIE: Why don't you stay in da back house? 'S yours, you know.
SPENCER: No, it belongs to you. I don't deserve it. I'll find my own place.
DEBBIE: You know wat? I'm not going to marry Jeremy and move to England. I'm not even going to da Middle East. I belong in Hawai'i. Hawai'i da bes'.
SPENCER: What happen?
DEBBIE: If Jeremy loves me, he can live in Hawai'i. I got things to do here. I realized it when I was wit' Mama and Laura today.
SPENCER: Like wat?
DEBBIE: I'm gonna stay here and take pictures of Hawai'i. Not da tourist kine wit' only scenery. But real pictures. Pictures of da people and all da different faces and colors. People working, playing, laughing, crying. Da dark side and da bright side. And someday I'm gonna publish 'um in a book.
SPENCER: Sounds exciting.

DEBBIE: I dunno wat I was thinking about. Everyting I want is right here. I don't have to go anywhere. I told Mama already.

SPENCER: She was happy, eh.

DEBBIE: Oh yeah. And, Spenca, I know deep in her heart, Mama happy you coming home.

SPENCER: I hope so. T'anks, Debbie.

(AKI *and* FUMIKO *enter.*)

AKI: Well, tonight I can get one good sleep.

FUMIKO: You wen' drink your medicine?

AKI: Oh, forget. (*Yelling offstage.*) Aeh, Toku, bring me one cup watta. Once in a while, I forget drink. You too?

FUMIKO: Sometimes.

AKI: Too much excitement today, 's why. Spenca, you gotta drink medicine like us?

SPENCER: Not yet.

AKI: Good. Take care of your body. You only get one. Your health da mos' important ting.

(TOKU *enters with the cup of water.*)

T'ank you. (*He swallows his pill with the water.*) Okay, now we can go.

FUMIKO: Toku, you going to da car?

TOKU: Yup.

FUMIKO: Mo' betta I go wit' you now.

TOKU: Okay.

SPENCER: Toku, you serious about opening a restaurant?

TOKU: Well, I was talking to Laura. Too young to retire, no mo' money, gotta do someting.

SPENCER: If I can help . . . if you let me, I got some money saved up. I can help you get started.

TOKU: Sure. I no mo' shame. I take all da help I can get.

SPENCER: Good. Thanks.

TOKU: By da way, I wish tings wen' betta wit' da company. You know, I wen' learn plenty from your faddah.

SPENCER: Open that restaurant. I'll be your first customer.

TOKU: Well, da firs' one might be small. Someting like Toku's Cafe. But if get popular, we might open up one branch, den one nodda one. For da grand opening, I might invite da governor to come taste my chicken heka, da Ariyoshi Special.

DEBBIE: We betta go, Toku.

TOKU: Okay.

(TOKU, DEBBIE, *and* FUMIKO *exit.*)

LAURA: (*Offstage.*) Toku! Toku!

AKI: You neva talk to Laura yet, eh?

SPENCER: No, why?

AKI: I not sticking around for dat. You on your own. Me chicken shit. Look out, she coming.

(AKI *hurries upstage by the bushes, hides, and listens.* LAURA *enters and sees only* SPENCER. *She folds the tablecloth and assembles the remaining items.*)

SPENCER: Laura. I said things I shouldn't have. I was confused. . . . Sorry.

(*She continues cleaning up silently.*)

I don't blame you for being mad at me. I acted pretty stupid. . . . Actually it was better that you helped Daddy with the business instead of me. I would've made Daddy's life miserable with my complaining. But you were different. You were great. Well, I just wanted to let you know. . . . (*He starts to leave.*)

LAURA: In a way . . . I was happy you went to the mainland. I loved working with Daddy. We shared so many things togedda. Lots of times afta work, he would brew some Kona coffee, and the two of us would sit in the office by ourselves just talking about the day's work. He loved his coffee. He put his feet on the desk and just relaxed. He neva went drinking with the boys afta work. He stayed in the office to talk with me. Those were the happiest times of my life. I think Daddy enjoyed talking to me too. I hope so.

SPENCER: I'm sure he did.

LAURA: Maybe I should thank you. If you had stayed home, then I would've have missed out on all those times with Daddy. Because he wouldn't have needed me then. He would've depended on you.

SPENCER: I don't know. Maybe not.

LAURA: I guess I sound selfish, but my days with Daddy is someting you can neva have. Daddy went out of his way to make me feel important, to make me feel appreciated. He was so good, and you neva really knew him. I'll always cherish my time with him.

SPENCER: I envy you. You deserve the good memories you have of Daddy. At least you didn't fail him like I did.

LAURA: But . . . I wasn't going to tell you this. Mama and Debbie don't know, not even Toku. But the night before Daddy passed away, he was dreaming or delirious. He was restless in bed. I was alone with him that time and I said, "Daddy, what's wrong? It's me, Laura." But all he said was, "Spenca, come help me. Spenca." I guess he was still thinking of you at the end.

(LAURA *exits.* AKI *peers out from the bush.*)

AKI: You folks had one good talk or wat?

SPENCER: You one big help, Uncle.

AKI: I tell you one ting. Wen you get old like me, you know wen to talk and wen to walk.

(MAX *and* DANIEL *enter.*)

Danny, you ready to go?

DANIEL: Anytime you are.

MAX: Look at dat sunset.

DANIEL: I don't think I'll see a more beautiful sunset anywhere.

AKI: You shoulda seen da one from da Kona coast wen I was one kid. Knock your eyes out. Well, Max, hope I see you again.

MAX: Oh yeah. Now dat Spenca returning, I going be hanging out wit him.

AKI: Good. I figga I going be around anodda twenty-five years, so get plenty time. I take you to da cockfights sometime.

MAX: It's a deal.

AKI: Yeah, I gotta live long enough to talk to Danny's children. 'S wat grandparents for, you know, to tell da kids wat life was like in da old days, so dey no forget where dey came from.

DANIEL: Grandpa, you give meaning to what Carl Jung once said.

AKI: Wat dat?

DANIEL: He said, "The afternoon of human life must also have a significance of its own and cannot be merely a pitiful appendage to life's morning."

(AKI *tries hard to conceal his puzzlement.*)

AKI: Carl Yung, eh? Yeah, he was one smart Chinese man. We go already. Tomorrow morning we gotta get two plumeria trees ready for Mrs. Wallace.

SPENCER: Take it easy, Danny.

DANIEL: Yeah, see you guys.

MAX: No shovel too much manure.

(DANIEL *exits.* AKI *is about to follow but stops.*)

AKI: I tell you one ting. Dat kid woulda made one tarrific nurseryman.

(*He cocks his head, smiles wistfully, then exits.*)

MAX: Well, brah, I hope you know wat you doing, coming back home.

SPENCER: Aeh, who knows. Kinda scary. But I gotta take the chance. I was missing something on the mainland. Maybe it's the way of life here. This is my last hope. Things gotta change for the better. If nuttin' else, at least I'll be back with my people and I'll have native soil between my toes again.

(*The stage darkens as the sun sinks into the ocean. The glow of the charcoal in the grill becomes brighter and is reflected on* SPENCER, *who stands behind the grill. The effect of the glow and the darkness on stage is one of serenity. A native son has returned home. Lights dim to black.*)

THE END

Glossary

The following words and phrases are from Japanese, Hawaiian, and Hawaiian Creole English (HCE). It was and is customary for many people to use them interspersed within English sentences.

abunai	dangerous
anshin	at peace
Ariyoshi Special	reference to George Ariyoshi, governor at the time, 1980
auwe (Hawaiian)	exclamation: that's terrible
baka	stupid, fool
bakatade	or bakatare; see baka
bambai (HCE)	by and by, later; or else
babasan	grandma
bā-san	old woman
benjo	toilet
bentō	lunch
bon	Buddhist celebration
bumbai (HCE)	see bambai
chotto	a little
dame, kore. Iran!	This is useless. I don't need it.
daijōbu	okay, alright
daikon	large, bulbous radish
dōmo arigatō	thank you
dō itashimashite	you're welcome
erai	weary

faka (HCE)	faker
gambare	persevere
gobo	burdock root
gomen; gomen nasai	excuse me
gottsosama	or gochisō-sama; thanks for the delicious meal
guzuguzu no you (Japanese and HCE)	so slow, you! you're so slow, aren't you!
hagamuge	toothless
hai	yes
halulu (Hawaiian)	haywire, crazy
haole (Hawaiian)	Caucasian, White
Hawai'i no ka oi (Hawaiian)	Hawai'i is the best
hayō	hurry up
hazukashii	embarrassed
heka (HCE)	shoyu-flavored stir-fried dish
hiza bonsan	lit. "knee priest"; ref. to kneecaps
hoe hana (HCE)	hoeing weeds; to weed with a hoe
hoito	greedy
honto	true
hybolic (HCE)	hyper-intellectual
ima	now
isogashii	busy
itai	hurt
jiichan	grandpa
jōdan da nai	don't joke with me
kālua (Hawaiian)	steamed in an underground oven
Kanaka (Hawaiian)	person, Native Hawaiian
kanshakumochi	cranky, ill-tempered
kapulu (Hawaiian)	messy
kau kau (HCE)	food; to eat
kawaigaru	to care for, affectionately
kawaii	cute
kawaisō	poor thing!
kichigai	crazy
kitanai	dirty
kobu	kelp
koshi ga itai	back hurts

kūkae (Hawaiian)	feces
Kumamoto	prefecture in Kyushu, Japan
kurō	hardship
lauhala (Hawaiian)	leaf of hala tree
laulau (Hawaiian)	food steamed in ti leaves
liliko'i (Hawaiian)	passion fruit
lōlō (Hawaiian)	crazy
ma-ke (Hawaiian)	die, dead
makule (Hawaiian)	old
malasadas (Portuguese)	Portuguese doughnuts
mempachi	red squirrel fish
mimi-kuso	ear wax
miso	soy-bean paste
mitemi	take a look
moe lepo (Hawaiian)	really dirty; expression of disgust
monkutade	whiner, complainer
musubi	rice ball
namasu	vinegared vegetables
nandai	what's going on?
nani	what
nebosuke	sleepyhead
niga-haru	too much; excessive
nishime	boiled, seasoned stew
nonkena	easygoing
nonki	easygoing
obake	ghost
ogo	seaweed
oishii	delicious
okaeri	welcome home
okashii	strange, funny
okāsan	mother
'ōkole (Hawaiian)	rear end
okusan	Mrs.
'ōno (Hawaiian)	delicious
oshiri	rear end
otōsan	father
oyakōkō	filial piety
pau (Hawaiian)	finish

pīkake (Hawaiian)	jasmine flower
pilikia (Hawaiian)	trouble
pohā (Hawaiian)	fruit
pohō (Hawaiian)	waste
potot (HCE)	tiny; from "small potatoes"?
puka (Hawaiian)	hole
pupule (Hawaiian)	crazy
saimin (HCE)	local noodle dish in hot broth
senkō	incense
shaka (HCE)	sharp, terrific
shiishii	urine, urinate
shōganai	or shikata ga nai; can't be helped
tedesuke	stupid; a fool
tempura	deep-fried fish and vegetables
tōchan	diminutive, slang for otōsan
uji (HCE)	slimy, creepy
ume-boshi	pickled plum
unko	feces
urusai	bothersome
wahine (Hawaiian)	female, woman
warui	bad
yakamashii	noisy
ya-re ya-re	expression of weariness: good grief
yō nitoru	or yoku nite iru; really resembles
yonsei	fourth generation Japanese American
yōshi	adopted child
zabuton	seat cushion

ABOUT THE AUTHOR

EDWARD SAKAMOTO has written thirteen plays, eight of which have Hawai'i themes. His plays have been staged in such places as Los Angeles, New York City, San Francisco, Stockton, and Hawai'i. He received Po'okela Awards for *Aloha Las Vegas* and *Our Hearts Were Touched with Fire* and Hollywood Drama-Logue Critics Awards for *Chikamatsu's Forest* and *Stew Rice*. In 1988 he was honored with a Los Angeles County Proclamation from the Board of Supervisors commending his contributions to theater. He has received a Rockefeller American Playwrights in Residence Award, a National Endowment for the Arts grant, and another Rockefeller grant.

Mr. Sakamoto graduated from 'Iolani High School in 1958 and received a B.A. degree in English at the University of Hawai'i in 1962. He has worked as a copy editor at the *Los Angeles Times* and is a member of the Dramatists Guild.

Production Notes

Composition and paging were done using
FrameMaker 4.0 for Windows by the design
and production staff of University of
Hawai'i Press.

The text typeface is Goudy Old Style
and the display typeface is Eras.

www.ingramcontent.com/pod-product-compliance
Lightning Source LLC
Chambersburg PA
CBHW032257150426
43195CB00008BA/488